Robert Frost

and John Bartlett

Robert Frost
and John Bartlett

The Record of a Friendship

by Margaret Bartlett Anderson

———————

HOLT, RINEHART AND WINSTON

New York   Chicago   San Francisco

Published simultaneously in Canada by Holt, Rinehart
and Winston of Canada, Limited.

Library of Congress Catalog Card Number: 63-17027

First Edition

Grateful acknowledgment is made to Holt, Rinehart and
Winston, Inc., for permission to reprint several poems
from *Complete Poems of Robert Frost,* copyright, 1923,
1928, 1934 by Holt, Rinehart and Winston, Inc., copyright
renewed 1951, © 1956, 1962 by Robert Frost; and from
In the Clearing by Robert Frost, copyright © 1962 by
Robert Frost.

Designer: Ernst Reichl
80404-0113
Printed in the United States of America

To the memory of my father and mother,
John T. and Margaret A. Bartlett;
and to my children,
Bart, Kathy, David, Debby,
Chris, and Molly.

Contents

Preface

ROBERT FROST first requested that the letters to John Bartlett, written "in the simplicity of the heart back there when none of us was anybody," be kept a private matter until after his death. When my parents died, John Bartlett in 1947 and Margaret Abbott Bartlett in 1949, the letters were passed to me with instructions to "do something" with them before placing the collection in a library for permanent keeping. Eventually there comes a time to let go of old and cherished memories. In the dedication of Frost's book, *In The Clearing*, he gave his permission:

> Letters in prose to
> Louis Untermeyer, Sidney Cox, and John Bartlett
> for them to dispose of as they please; . . .

The collection of letters, some sixty in all, dating back to 1912, had their importance to Frost as Poet; but the significance to me has always been the story behind the letters, Frost as Friend.

My first awareness of Frost was in terms of "making a difference" in our house. He was the one person whose presence could silence the typewriters in "the office," the focal room of the Bartlett house. From infancy, when my mother would soothe my restlessness by holding me across her knees as she typed, the clickity-click of typewriters was the steady rhythm of our home in Boulder, Colorado. Few outsiders came into our lives. The mailman was the pipeline of all activity, bringing stacks of letters daily: long fat envelopes containing manuscripts and long thin ones from editors. Piles of trade journals covered desk surfaces and overflowed into closets, in corners, and on the floor under the desks. Thumbing through *Furniture Age*, *Boot and Shoe Recorder*, or *The Flower Grower* in search of pictures to cut out or color, I might find articles by John T. or Margaret A. Bartlett, but the text hardly matched Grimms' fairy tales.

I was eight when Robert and Elinor Frost first visited us in 1931. My brothers and I were told that "Rob" was a very famous poet, an exciting prospect, but he only looked like a grandfather I'd never known. Most impressive, he was the first "friend" ever invited to stay overnight in our home. The typewriters, the pulse of the house, were muted in his honor, shut off behind an office door which had never been closed before in my memory. When I was in high school, the only excuse ever written for me to be absent from school for any reason other than illness, was to accompany my parents to Denver to meet

Frost at the railroad station. We went to a hotel near the station and sat in the lobby for a two-hour talk between trains. My parents' response to Frost was an immediate pushing aside of all other considerations. When his daughter Marjorie came as a patient to the tuberculosis sanitarium three blocks from our house, the whole family took her in. She gave me my first vision of young womanhood, and, later, my first experience with death; death of someone I knew, someone who was not old or ready to die.

After her long day at the office desk, my mother would talk to me in the kitchen while she sliced boiled potatoes for a "left-over" supper. As the youngest of four, but more likely because I was the only girl, she would tell me stories of her past, her dreams, her love of poetry. Few stories pre-dated her Pinkerton Academy years, as if her awareness of herself did not begin until she met my father in Frost's classroom. Young love blossomed there; and Frost had nurtured her pleasure in poetry and in writing. She was sentimental, holding the past like a crystal prism from an antique chandelier and telling me the stories over and over again.

I never saw my father read a book of poetry. I never heard him talk about Frost. Sometimes, in a playing-hooky kind of mood, he'd leave an unfinished cylinder on the dictaphone in his upstairs office and invite me to go fishing with him up Boulder Canyon. As a fisherman, he looked inappropriately businesslike, standing on a rock in Boulder Creek with the erect posture and the intense look of an after-dinner speaker, dressed in an old but tolerably pressed suit, with a respectable straw hat on his head. My father never caught a trout on these occasions.

His fly-casting was a little absent-minded, and he'd likely snare an aspen branch, the limb of a fir, or hook a log wedged between boulders in the icy stream. But we both understood that we weren't really after fish. Our catch for the day was the sound of cold, tumbling creek water, the wind in the upper branches of the Colorado blue spruce, and the smell of freshly showered mountains. Colorado climate was something to *know*, like the New England climate of John's boyhood, the setting of his friendship with Robert Frost.

The first time I ever saw the collection of Frost letters, although I'd heard them mentioned, was when my mother discovered mice nesting in the bottom drawer of the Winthrop desk in the dining room. Nothing mattered but the battered manila envelope, anxiously removed and its contents spread on the dining table to check the damage. Only the English periodical, *Poetry and Drama*, a Christmas gift from Frost in December, 1913, was gnawed at the edges, destroying some of the marginal notations. I don't remember what happened to the mice, but the letters were placed in another used manila envelope and returned to the drawer. Except for members of the family, no one saw the letters.

I didn't know until after my father died that there were also pages and pages of "Notes on Conversations," written after each of Frost's visits in the thirties. Judging from my father's almost illegible handwriting, they were written in great haste, the spilling out of a whole evening's talk. In telling me about the "Notes," my mother puzzled, "I wonder what John meant to do with them," for he apparently never discussed with her any plans to write the story of the friendship. He never talked about it, and almost furtively stuffed the notes in a folder in the office filing cabinet. The notes are curious, in a way. As if standing at a distance, my father records Frost's talk, activities, and moods with great objectivity and conscientious detail. Ordinarily, as a writer who had received his training as a newspaper reporter, his notes were highly selective, usually dictated for the secretary to transcribe. Nobody had read these "Notes," not even my mother, although she knew what they were. At various points my father asks questions—"What accounts for this change [in Frost] . . . ?"—questions directed, it seems, to himself, as if he sought an understanding of this man whom he regarded as a master of situations and insight. My guess is that my father had in mind to write something about Frost as he knew him, but posthumously. He was careful never to use his friendship with Frost to further any self-interest—except when he asked him to write a recommendation for me when I applied for admission to Wellesley College.

After my father's death the letters assumed a precious importance to my mother for the memories they contained, particularly the stories relating to her courtship with my father and the early years of her marriage. She planned to publish the letters, and talked more and more of writing the story as her physical strength gave way before cancer. Her plan for publishing the letters was blocked by Frost's denying his permission, requesting that the privacy of the letters be preserved during his lifetime. When she died, the letters were willed to me, along with the privilege of telling the story.

I have not attempted to write the account as either my father or mother might have written it. Much was lost

with them, but the record of the friendship, the length
and depth of it, emerges from the letters. The discovery
to me is seeing my parents as people, instead of as parents, and appreciating the quality of Frost's relationship
with them. *Knowing* Frost made a difference in the working out of their lives. This story, drawn from what was
told me, from the letters, which are quoted without
amending the spelling or punctuation, and the "Notes on
Conversations," is my tribute to Robert Frost and to my
parents, John and Margaret Bartlett.

—M.B.A.

Robert Frost

and John Bartlett

I

Egg Man in Derry

In his poem, "New Hampshire," Robert Frost tells that when he left Massachusetts for the Derry farm, he had no expectations of finding friends the equal of those he'd already known, but in time he changed his mind.

> I hadn't an illusion in my hand-bag
> About the people being better there
> Than those I left behind. I thought they weren't.
> I thought they couldn't be. And yet they were.
> I'd sure had no such friends in Massachusetts
> As Hall of Windham, Gay of Atkinson,
> Bartlett of Raymond (now of Colorado),
> Harris of Derry, and Lynch of Bethlehem.

The friends he found were not there to greet him in 1900 when Robert Frost, with his wife Elinor and daughter Lesley, moved into the farm on the Windham Road, two miles down the turnpike from Derry, New Hampshire. Neighbors thought he "looked sickly," and he was. Frost had left Harvard feeling a sickness in his heart or his stomach or his lungs, somewhere inside, deep inside, and a doctor had warned that the illness might be tuberculosis. Elinor, grieving the loss of their firstborn son, Eliot, feared another loss. She talked her father-in-law into buying a farm for them, one of the many small Rockingham County farms on the kind of land an early chronicler had joked about as, "the more you owned, the poorer you'd likely be." For $1,800 they owned a house, pasture, orchard, and spring. Although they were strangers to Derry, the farm was only twelve miles from Lawrence where Frost had attended high school and where he had met Elinor White. She had shared valedictory honors with him and later become his wife. The three sought a snug, close warmth, with the somewhat practical thought of raising chickens and selling eggs to meet their needs.

Frost, reminiscing about those years on the Windham Road farm, describes the life they made for themselves:

"For six months after we went to the farm, I did nothing. The rugs were there, but I didn't put them down. The well was only twenty or thirty steps from the door. It would have been a simple thing to have piped it into the house, but during the entire eight years there we carried water. There was always a bucket in the sink.

"I was ambition-less, purposeless. For months on end I would do no work at all. I didn't write because I wanted to write. I wrote because I wrote. I would exchange work with another farmer, perhaps, during the haying, and for three weeks would sweat and toughen up. Then the hay fever would come on, and I would do no work until another haying.

"During the entire eight years there no friend ever sat down within our home. I'd have conversations from time to time with a trader interested in buying or selling a horse, or a poultry buyer. Friends never came. There were no friends. I sometimes think of those years as almost a fadeout . . . as an escape into a dream existence. . . ."

And yet he was aware of the town, the people. Derry had its farms, many as marginal as his own, but it was an industrial town, too. There were several small shoe factories, but the native pride in Yankee resourcefulness and ingenuity was reflected more in the local Chase woodworking mill. The mill still operates, a surviving industry, turning out gross quantities of small wood products: tongue blades used by doctors and the small wooden tags nurserymen use to label plants. About all that could be said of Frost's productivity was his increase in children: Carol, a son, and two more daughters, Irma and Marjorie, born on the farm. By the local measure of things he was regarded as "something of a failure," giving townspeople little more for his being there than an object to criticize. Frost heard what they said:

"Hen Shute once said to Carl Burrell (hired man), 'I hear he's well-educated, too.' And Carl said, 'He never earned over ten dollars a week in his life.' And it was true."

Henry Shute was a villager who worked in the kitchen

of his wife's boarding house—likely never made a dollar a week himself—but anyone can say anything and be right, too, if that means anything. There was much in the social contacts of these early years to embarrass and humiliate Frost, but he made no defense. He simply bore the weight of social disapproval. Frost went away from people on the Windham Road farm, but he also returned to the world of people in Derry.

"We were in debt, and, somehow, coming to have a prejudice against debt. It occurred to us that I might take up teaching again. I went to Lawrence [where he had taught in his mother's school] and met on the street a minister named Wolcott, who'd taken a friendly interest in my mother and me years before. When my first poem was published [at seventeen] this minister sent for me, in part, I found, to congratulate me, but more to warn me. He was thinking of my mother. When I told him I was thinking of taking up teaching, he remarked there was an academy near me at Derry. He knew a minister who was one of the trustees, and he promised to write him."

The minister was Charles Merriam, pastor of the Central Congregational Church, Trustee of Pinkerton Academy, and influential in Derry affairs.

"When I found Merriam, he was busy drilling a troop of boys and he kept me waiting nearly an hour, standing against a wall. When we began to talk, I could see he was suspicious. He rolled his wall eyes at me in a cautious way."

There must have been salesmanship involved, for it was true that Frost had "run away" from both Dartmouth and Harvard without benefit of a degree. His

6

teaching experience was limited to his mother's school
and two or three terms in other schools. But he had
wares: he had some poetry, and the Reverend Merriam
was sufficiently impressed to invite Rob to read a poem
at the Men's League of the Congregational Church. It
was to be an evening meeting with important Derry
citizens present: John C. Chase, Trustee of Pinkerton
and head of the local mill, and Charles Abbott, another
Trustee and State Senator. Such a gathering was more
than Frost could face, but Mr. Merriam offered to read
the poem. With grave misgivings for leaving his wife
alone (only twice in eight years had he been away from
Elinor in the evening), the arrangements were made.

"A Tuft of Flowers" was the offering, written for the
occasion and read as a bid for a teaching position, "as
little Tommy Tucker sang for his supper." On the
strength of the poem, he was offered a part-time position
teaching English at Pinkerton, which took him on at a
bargain price, one-sixth of a thousand dollars for the
year, to teach one class. "They got me cheap," Frost later
said, but he didn't haggle over the price. It was income.

The walk from his farm to Pinkerton was the same
distance for one class as it was later when he taught full-
time, a good two miles, partly hilly, crossing West-
running Brook before reaching Derry village. Pinkerton
Academy still stands on a hill overlooking the village, a
solidly built red-brick structure, properly symmetrical,
with a central tower. Just down the slope is the "old
Academy" building, austerely painted white, and as carefully preserved as the tradition of the school. Founded in
1815, the purpose of the Academy was "to promote piety

and virtue and the education of youth in Science, Languages, and the Liberal Arts."

Head of the school was George Washington Bingham, aged principal and Latin scholar, whose dignity measured up to his imposing 6′ 4″ height. His rules for behavior were as strict as those governing declensions and conjugations. If Frost had ever attended required morning chapel, he would have heard the reading of "Requirements": "Any student who wastes time in trifling amusements or is untruthful or disobedient or neglects studies or in any way exerts an influence unfavorable to the good name and usefulness of the school, will be deprived of its privileges." Students were to be in their homes or dormitory at 7:00 P.M. and not leave thereafter, except Friday evening when grace was extended to 10:00 P.M. and Sunday evening when they were expected to attend church services. Once a week the principal called the roll of the assembled student body (about 120 in all), and each student reported his record of the week: "All the requirements," "one exception, excused," "two requirements." Discipline, hard work, and no nonsense; the beginning and end of a sound Christian education.

In 1906 Frost entered the scene, not at a decorous walk, and never in time for chapel, but often at a gallop, taking the steps two at a time to reach his class. His hair, cut at home, was blown in all directions by the wind, and if that weren't enough, he'd run his fingers through the tousled locks defying any accidental order. His clothes were rumpled and ill-fitting. There were no indications that he made any effort to "spruce up" for the job. In class, unlike the ramrod-straight Miss Parsons who

8

taught Greek or the stiff-collared Art Reynolds who taught history, Frost would slump down in his chair behind his desk, almost disappearing from sight except for his heavy-lidded eyes and bushy brows. In such a position Frost would "talk," or he might read aloud or let a discussion go its own length. Teachers didn't know how to "take him," and students, accustomed to "prepared lessons," were inclined to think they could take advantage of a teacher who was not strict in the way they knew.

Frost felt his first year of teaching a failure. The year ended with his leaving before finishing the spring term because of pneumonia and hay fever, an illness which nearly consumed him, as it also consumed most of the salary he made that year. Harder to bear than the physical strain of teaching was the hostility he felt from other members of the faculty and his students. When upperclassmen were asked to submit to Frost their arguments for a debate between the Junior and Senior students (in the order of classes: Junior, Junior Middler, Senior Middler, and Senior), the Seniors refused. They may have simply felt the cockiness of a sure win, but, for whatever reason, it was a defiant act. Such disobedience would ordinarily have merited a rebuke from the principal. None came. There was no support for Frost. It was a public debate, so crowded with townspeople that students sat under the window ledges and on the mantle. When the Juniors won the debate, beating out the Seniors for the first time in the history of Pinkerton inter-class debates, Frost felt they'd evened a score for him. The class of 1910 was thereafter *his* class.

In spite of his feelings of failure, Frost was asked back the next year to take on a second class. He dared not risk teaching until the first freeze cleared the air of plaguing pollens. Starting the school year late, he found his classes had been shunted into the principal's office because of overcrowding. Two new students had joined the Junior Middler class in the fall of 1907. John Bartlett, a boarding student from Raymond, New Hampshire, sat among the boys in front of Frost; Margaret Abbott, from Derry Depot, sat with the girls at right angles to the boys.

Whatever feelings Frost had of townfolk or faculty hostility, they had no place in his classroom. Students who were familiar with his ways, and the two new pupils, accepted him for what he was. Instead of being discouraged from studies by his easy manner of reading aloud and his casual talk, Frost's students used this greater freedom to work harder. He did assign themes, contrary to later stories about his teaching methods, and any student willing to work would find helpful comments in the margin of his paper: "There, you have found the kind of thing you can do." "This really is an idea. The occasion is splendid. This seems to be done from life. What an interesting runaway." He'd ask questions as if he could learn something from them, an astonishing attitude for a teacher to take.

For the students who held his interest, the ones who responded, like John Bartlett and Margaret Abbott, the formal classroom was almost incidental. Frost was often "around," watching the boys work out on the football field after school. Sometimes he'd take off his coat and "make a bluff" at playing ball, to the amusement of the boys. On one occasion he noticed John Bartlett standing near him and casually asked him some questions about a theme he'd submitted describing the Devil's Den, a rock formation in the Pawtuckaway mountains, where John spent his summers on the family farm.

"I answered them awkwardly," John wrote of the meeting. "I was a shy boy. In a matter of fact way Frost observed that I was a fellow who had ideas. That's all there was to the conversation, as a spinning ball came my way, but I can see Frost, the fall mud, and the football bucking machine. . . . He seemed to have several times the interest in me that other teachers had."

Gradually, this intensely personal, though never hurried, interest drew out the students, and Frost's judgment won their respect. An "A" from Frost became a coveted honor. The athlete of the '10 class, Dave Griffith, a magnificent half-back and hundred-yarder, generally had a haughty disregard for scholastic honors (few of which he ever received), but an "A" on a theme (athletic in subject) from Frost was different. Breaking the study-hour rule of the dormitory, Dave stealthily went from room to room to announce his achievement grandly. Whatever merit a boy had, Frost was able to find it sooner or later.

He'd walk with John Bartlett down the country roads, covering a world of subjects in just a mile. If they came abreast of a logging team, Frost would stop and talk with the teamster about logging things, horses, and roads. Once they walked to Manchester, browsed for an hour in a bookstore, and then, fortifying themselves with oyster stew, rode the electric railway back to Derry. If the daylight ran out and the stars shone through the trees, it might be the occasion to discuss astronomy or Greek mythology; noticing a fern, Frost might observe that he hadn't seen one like it since he was last in the Lake Willoughby region; talk might be of present things, like baseball and football; or something could touch off reminiscences of his boyhood in industrial Lawrence. Rob never argued. He knew what he knew. And he would get his companion to talk, often about things he wasn't aware that he knew.

John knew the New Hampshire woods. The Pawtuckaway mountains were rich with a boy's knowledge of what the land held. As soon as school was out in the summer, John would go to the farm with his mother, older sisters, Bess and Ada, and younger brother, Bob. The house was always in need of repairs and isolated from neighbors. Except for haying, summer was a season of days to fill up with whatever the boys could find to do. In a single day John and Bob could catch a hundred fish in Round Pond—pickerel, perch, and pout. Cleaning was not as much fun as catching the fish, but the jackknife was always honed sharp, for it was the indispensable tool of a New England boy. John learned the trees by the feel of his knife cutting the wood, whittling wooden chains, willow whistles, trick boxes, and acorn cups. Exploring the mountains to reach the nearly inaccessible Devil's Den, John and Bob might spot a hive of honey bees, and, going back after dark, they'd chop the hive open and gather pails of wild honey. They always tried to catch the queen, with thought of starting their own swarm and going into the honey business, but were never successful. The boys had better luck snaring rabbits for a succulent dinner, catching squirrels for pets—and turtles and frogs.

John knew where to find the best walnuts, the most tender checkerberry leaves, and cooling twigs of birchbark. Cowslip greens, bitter to his adult taste, and the rock-hard hickory nuts he was unable to crack in later years always remained sweet taste treats in John's nostalgic memory of New Hampshire woods.

If bad weather kept the boys confined, John would browse through dusty books, odd volumes often picked up by his father at auctions. Copies of *The American Boy* and *The Youth's Companion* were stacked in piles to be read and re-read, year after year. The older sisters, Ada and Bess, turned their dramatic flair into writing stories for contests in the Boston *Globe*.

On weekends John's father would drive to the farm in the horse and wagon to see how things were going. John T., Sr., was a soft-spoken, dignified gentleman with a heavy mustache, a small-town lawyer who'd first taught school, then "read the law" at night in order to enter the profession. "Well, Old Hundred," he'd say affectionately to one of his sons after a chore had been done, "Shall I pay you now or shall I mark it in the book?" The dutiful son would reply, "Mark it in the book, Papa," and the three cents would be carefully added to a column of figures in the ledger. It was a thrifty Yankee maneuver, since the boys never collected their accumulated earnings, but it looked very grown up and business-like. The column of figures in a bank book was always important to John.

But the dynamic force of the Bartlett household was John's mother, Emma Lake Tucker, from up Deerfield way. She'd been a schoolteacher in Raymond before marrying John T. Bartlett, and, after her four children were born, helped the family finances by taking in boarders.

As Frost discovered when he came for supper, the Bartlett boarding house had a reputation, but not for cooking or housekeeping. No scullery maid, "Mother Bartlett" had other things to offer: talk, conversation, and interest in people. She taught her boarders, often immigrants who came to work in the shoe factory in Raymond, how to speak English, read good books, and encouraged them to do something better than menial job-holding with their lives. Jimmy Pappadim, a Greek, became a permanent boarder, and after one failure in business became the owner of a chain of three candy stores. Angelo Nappi, a scrappy Italian boy, came to Raymond knowing little more than slang and swear words and how to defend himself with a knife. Through Mother Bartlett's influence, and with Bess to teach him English, he became a highly literate and skilled barber. "Truly a metamorphosis," he wrote of the change in his ways after his association with the Bartlett household. Not all Mother Bartlett's efforts produced winners, however. One boarder seriously embarked on a home-study program, buying an encyclopedia on the installment plan, one volume at a time. A to L was enough. He left the unfinished set in lieu of rent.

Mother Bartlett would feed tramps or "gentlemen wanderers," as she'd sometimes call them, glad to give a free meal if they had a good story to tell. Politics, literature, anything could be a topic for discussion. Though no suffragette ("I'm busy tending children," she once told a petitioner), she was, in the early twenties when she was widowed, one of the first women elected to the New Hampshire State Legislature—on the Democratic ticket. In her maiden speech she made headlines when she put an admiral to rout, a feat described in the newspapers as "the most brilliant fireworks of the session." People in Raymond weren't surprised. Mother Bartlett had a great heart, a woman's heart, but she could talk as well as a man on any subject.

John grew up close to his mother in ways of talk; and his eye for detail, his quick ability to grasp an idea, and his intense, probing interest in almost any subject were a delight to Frost. And John would listen to the older man with an instinctive knowledge that Frost was a good measure above any other teacher he had ever known.

John also had—in addition to his consuming interest in football, baseball, and track—an eye for Margaret Abbott. She looked taller than she was, a slim graceful figure of a girl with an abundance of fine brown hair, brushed and tied with a satin bow at the back of her neck. Her hands were small as a child's, with slender, tapered fingers capable of the finest of needlework. Margaret was sweet and winsome, always ready with a smile, but serious and hard-working, too. When she caught John looking at her, her white skin would flush a warm pink, and her eyes would shine a little brighter when she'd look again to be sure John had picked her out. She worried that people would notice the quivering petals of the rose pinned to her blouse, which betrayed her fluttering heart beneath.

The themes she wrote for Frost always came back with an "A." Being asked to express her thoughts, her feelings was like being invited to dance, and she wrote with care and delight. She seemed to come alive in front of Frost's eyes—and John's. The two "top pupils" were soon paired, together in all the odd moments that could be managed in the course of the day. Frost took pleasure in watching their shy and tenderly serious early love, mindful perhaps of his own love for Elinor White, the smartest girl in *his* high-school class.

Sometimes he'd walk with John and Margaret to the Abbott house in Derry Depot. He'd always be invited in and offered winter Baldwins or some of Ma Abbott's cream puffs, with a thick creamy custard filling that would ooze out at the first bite into the flaky crust. Ma Abbott was a thrifty New England housewife who kept hens for "egg money," but always saw to it that there were plenty of eggs left over to go into the rich baking for her family. Pa Abbott, a jovial, auburn-haired shoe factory foreman, would light up his after-dinner cigar, often with a twinkle in his eye. As a young girl Margaret had been seriously influenced by a temperance sermon at the Methodist church. She immediately went on strike, refusing to sit at the supper table until her father gave up drinking beer with his meal. She won that round, but Albert Abbott refused to give up his cigars.

Margaret had two older brothers, but both were away from home working in shoe factories by the time the Abbott family moved to Derry from Windsor, Vermont. As a little girl she'd had some serious illness, perhaps rheumatic fever, which had restricted her life to quiet pastimes: embroidery and visiting "shut-ins." She had the reputation of being the neighborhood "sunshine girl," seeking out the old ladies, the lonely ones, to give a bit of herself. She always said it was "Dandy Jack" who gave her "the taste of printer's ink." He was a little old man, a typesetter by trade, who lived down the lane from the Abbotts' in Windsor. When seen on the street he walked so erect that people said he wore a broomstick fastened to his backbone. But when Margaret would sometimes slip down the dark steps to his basement shop under the stationer's store, she'd find him sitting on a high stool and wearing a green eyeshade, humped over like a little gnome, with eyes moving as fast as his lightning-quick fingers, picking type from boxes. When she'd visit him, he'd set her name in type and print several cards for her to take home. She treasured the ink-smirched bits of cardboard, and would smudge her nose sniffing the pleasing aroma of printer's ink.

On the whole she felt boys were rough and rather mean; she'd had her long hair pulled and had been pushed in mud puddles. One Fourth of July, though, as she wrote in a poem, she'd huddled close to her mother by an upstairs window, listening to the celebration outside: firecrackers, the smell of punk, the rose light of the big bonfire, guns booming, drunks singing "How Dry I Am"—the excitement and recklessness of the men and boys celebrating the Fourth in turn-of-the-century style. Oh to be a boy on such a day!

But, mostly, Margaret had delicate tastes, and, although the schoolmarms openly disapproved of such recklessness among the girl pupils, she wore cotton undies instead of winter woolens. She was even daring enough to wear the popular "peekaboo" blouses that showed pretty pink and blue ribbon run through the lace of the corset covers underneath. In classes, Frost's readings from literature, particularly poetry, carried her aloft; and her world was one of delicate colors, quietness of voice, softness of touch, and tenderness of feelings. She suffered when she was a guest at John's house, where noisy discussions ("We never *argue*," said Mother Bartlett. "We *discuss!*") were always carried on with tempers rising, voices growing louder, and a hand banging on the table to drive home a point. Even John offended her when once, on one of their walks through the woods in search of ferns, they stopped by a dark mountain pond. In a romantic mood she asked John to pluck a bouquet of golden-hearted water lilies. She received instead, John being still boy, a lapful of baby turtles!

Once, her Methodist conscience bothered her. Young love, so painful and intense, seemed almost overwhelming, and she decided she was too young to be so deeply in love. For a whole week she avoided John, looking at him, if at all, from a cool distance. John, unable to understand any reason for such behavior, was in a torment, as his roommate or anyone else could tell. Frost watched the goings on: Margaret's unhappy aloofness and John's abject misery. A week was all he could tolerate. Taking Margaret aside, he said, "Go talk to John, Margaret. He's miserable!" She needed no more to erase all doubts from her mind. She never again questioned the rightness of her love for John, and with the joyous and snug feeling of being loved, worked harder than ever to be worthy of his love.

Frost's strength as a teacher gained momentum as his class "grew up" with him. Each year he was asked back, taking on more classes and trying new things. He directed four plays, but not the traditional Shakespeare. He chose, instead, Yeats' *The Land of Heart's Desire* and *Cathleen ni Houlihan*, Milton's *Comus*, and Marlowe's *Dr. Faus-*

tus. Margaret's favorite was *The Land of Heart's Desire,*
the lyrical Irish tale that begins with the bitter tongue
of the mother-in-law berating her son's wife:

> Because I bid her clean the pots for supper
> She took that old book down out of the thatch;
> She has been doubled over it ever since.

Outwardly quiet, Margaret, with a dancing fluttering
heart inside, felt a kinship with the mystic spirit of Mary,
and never forgot the lines:

> Faeries, come take me out of this dull world,
> For I would ride with you upon the wind,
> (Run on top of the dishevelled tide,)
> And dance upon the mountains like a flame.

More to John's taste was *Dr. Faustus.* He was the high-
stepping Mephistophilis whose lively dance portraying
the devil was not due as much to native talent as burning
himself snuffing out the candles with his bare fingers.

Everybody enjoyed the plays—Frost, the students, and
the townspeople. Frost even won support in unexpected
quarters. Mr. Bingham, admired for his sense of decorum,
stopped Frost on the street one day when he heard
Comus was to be presented. He offered the suggestion
that if Frost needed a silver service for Circe's banquet
scene, why he might use the church communion silver.
Frost was amused. "There seemed nothing out of the way
to him in using the communion service of the Congregational church for Circe's banquet."

Frost became the faculty advisor for *The Pinkerton
Critic,* the school's literary magazine. Under his "hands

off" policy of supervision the magazine gained a reputation among the schools of the state. Often, the articles written by John Bartlett, who was editor in his Senior year, were picked up by other school magazines to be quoted in the exchange columns. Each time a new issue came out Frost would discuss it with his classes; he was quite philosophical when an article appeared that wouldn't have passed for publication if it had been reviewed before printing. He could allow a student to fail without condemnation. He wrote on the blackboard the formula, famous with his classes, for the kind of matter used for literary purposes:

Uncommon in experience — uncommon in writing
Common in experience — common in writing
Uncommon in experience — common in writing
Common in experience — uncommon in writing

The last was the kind of material to search for, he told them.

The old order at Pinkerton was changing, and, though not intending any revolution, Frost's success in his English classes probably had something to do with the rapidity and completeness of the change. In 1909 the much-respected "Pa" Bingham retired, to be replaced by Ernest L. Silver, a "public-school man." He was short, blond, pink-cheeked, with a great deal of tact, not quite so much principle. New teachers, new courses were added: Domestic Science and Agriculture, with more up-to-date emphasis on "practical learning." Mr. Silver immediately put his Domestic Science department to good use, offering a faculty-prepared dinner to the football team after the big game of the season, Pinkerton vs. Sanborn Seminary, with cake and ice cream if the boys won.

John was Captain of the football team that fall, helping to shape a new squad of players. Frost would watch John playing his heart out on the cold, wet football field, making up in spirit what he lacked in build. John was just average height, inclined to breathe hard with his mouth open, his expression intent, all-absorbed in the play. His finely shaped hands, which sometimes gestured nervously when he was talking, could grip a football, hang onto a pass, or throw hard and accurately.

The final game with Sanborn Seminary was the kind of game a football player never forgets: air chill, rivalry hot, the score close, with Pinkerton driving to pull ahead in the final minutes. Those were the days when flying tackles were legal, and players wore broad belts so that backfielders could pick up the ball carrier by the belt and shoulders and push him through the wall of opposing players. It was on just such a line play that Duffy Doe of the Seminary, untangling himself from the heap of players, caught sight of John still holding the ball. In the heat of the moment he let fly with his fist to John's face. Teammates held Doe's arms, while John, with blood streaming down his cheek from a cut over his eye, called the next play—and drove through for a winning touchdown!

The victory dinner for the winning team and its wounded Captain was a sweet satisfaction, with steaming oyster stew, garlands of spicy sausages, potatoes, and the promised ice cream. Frost led the cheering with a string of verses he wrote on the blackboard, one of which was the chant:

In the days of Captain John,
Sanborn Sem had nothing on
Pinker-ton, Pinker-ton.

John and Margaret were closest to Frost, but he had
the respect and support of all the students by 1909. He
was then teaching full-time, still not attending chapel
(for fear of being called on to speak), still "ungroomed,"
to the despair of the Reverend Merriam. He still carried
the feeling that the faculty "wanted me out." When Mr.
Silver invited a group of inspectors from the state Board
of Education to visit his English class, Frost was sure that
this would be the end of his teaching career. "But," as
he told the story, "there was nothing to do but go ahead
as I always did. I could always count on John for a good
discussion, so I got him started. I kind of let him show me
off." The state inspectors stayed two hours. "I was sure
then they were going to put me out." Instead, he was
invited to speak at educational meetings throughout the
state. "I always felt I owed John something for that."

But early lectures were ordeals. Free and easy of
manner in the classroom, before an audience he suffered
agonies of apprehension. Once, he put pebbles in his
shoes and walked for an hour before he was to speak,
hoping the physical discomfort would relieve his anxieties.

Frost's class graduated in 1910, with Margaret Abbott
the undisputed honor student, the valedictorian. Frost
slipped the news to her before the faculty announcement,
then winked at John, saying with a shake of his head,
"Love and studies don't mix." Margaret felt grateful to
Frost—that he understood—but her uneasiness about
coming out ahead of John stayed with her. As she'd tell

the story, "and John came in second," which wasn't quite true. Another girl, Clarissa Hall, came in second, and John took third honors. But he was a three-letter man in athletics and class president his Senior year, enough for an outstanding record.

School days ended, although Frost remained for another year at Pinkerton, leaving the Windham Road farm to move into a house in Derry village not far from the Academy. Margaret took a position teaching six grades in a one-room school in Newton, New Hampshire. John, after studying shorthand and typing in the summer at a business school in Manchester, entered Middlebury College.

John's exposure to college was brief, ending before the first term was up. His thoughts were with Margaret, and the prospect of four years of college before marriage was intolerable. He could offer no reasonable solution, had no sense of "career" to somehow offset or hold in check his deep desire for Margaret. He developed severe bronchial asthma, which only added to the weight of his problems.

"I remember how I came down to Derry in late 1910, leaving college 'between two days,' defeated and defiant, meeting disapproval and condemnation, a boy who was getting hit by life and having no friendly overtures when he needed them most. And somehow Frost heard I was back, and walked miles to see me, and carry me out over the country roads for a friendly talk."

John's asthma had forced him to leave college before the end of the first term. Frost would see him from time to time, reckless of himself even when wheezing with asthma, tramping with wet feet over the hill toward Chester and Raymond.

Margaret would be home in Derry on weekends and would call on the Frosts. Her heart set for marriage, she enjoyed talking with Elinor, who was also shy and displayed a quiet concern and devotion for her husband. Margaret came to know the Frost children—Lesley, Carol, Irma, and Marjorie—youngsters who were charming, but unused to visitors.

In the duplex house with the Frosts lived a young couple, Lester Russell and his lovely wife from "near Boston." Lester's younger brother, Ivo, had been in John's class and would sometimes visit him at the Pawtuckaway farm. Margaret would see Mrs. Russell when she visited the Frosts, romantically eyeing the "ideal young married" couple. Lester was handsome, stunningly dressed, with a pleasing personality, trying to make his way as a young attorney in Derry and give his wife whatever she wanted. His low income was not enough for such standards of finery as he bought to please his wife or in order to appear prosperous himself. The story is told that he embezzled funds in such an open way he was bound to be caught. When, in due course, he was found out and served with a warrant for his arrest, Lester politely excused himself to get his coat. He took the opportunity to drink some Paris green and was dead by the following morning.

Frost was visiting John at the Pawtuckaway farm when word reached him. In the buggy on the way back to Derry he said, "Lester was the one person in Derry I got along with best." It was a simple, shocking tragedy, with public opinion blaming the outsider, the "city girl" wife whose tastes were beyond the means of her husband. Elinor and Margaret shared a heartfelt concern for Mrs.

Russell, left alone to work out her life, the worst possible fate Margaret could imagine. A wife must be careful not to ask too much of her husband, she thought.

By the end of the summer of 1911, before Frost left with his family for Plymouth where he was to teach "for one year" at Plymouth Normal School, John had decided to go to Vancouver, British Columbia, to try to regain his health. His sister Bess was living there with her husband, and a change of climate seemed the only hope at the moment. Frost "speeded me on my way to British Columbia, with a handshake, a look in the eye. There was a book at that parting—Chesterton's *Heretics*. I read it through three times on the way out." This was G. K. Chesterton, the portly Englishman who made a game of turning things upside down: "nothing fails like success" and "only the weak can be strong."

II

Vancouver,
1911-1914

In nineteen-ten
Vancouver then
Will have one hundred thousand men.
Move her! Move her!
Who?—Vancouver.

BY THE time John Bartlett arrived from New Hampshire
in the city "destined to become the Liverpool of Canada,"
Vancouver had outdistanced the promoters with a zoom-
ing population of 110,000. Dust of the Klondike still
settling, ships now unloaded treasures of raw silk and tea
to be hustled across Canada on fast Canadian and Pacific
freights to Montreal, New York, and London. Timber

was shipped to the Orient, canned salmon to all parts of the British Empire; and investors came from the United States, Belgium, France, and Germany to tap the wealth of timber, minerals, and rich farm land. The young city of scarcely one generation was expanding with the vigor, optimism, and recklessness of youth.

Land! The rush was on, more feverish than in the Yukon, with three real-estate offices for every grocery store. There were stories a'plenty of "the lot bought for $5,500 in 1899, and sold for $100,000 in 1911!" This was pioneer West, but still "British" British Columbia, with the cool humor of a newspaper cartoon noting that "speculators, with the connivance of the government, sometimes get their land for a dollar and a drink, and sometimes for a dollar without a drink." There was the hustle of the city, but in the background was the steady flowing of the Fraser river, the regularity of the tides in Burrard Inlet, the unmoving mountains, wild and wonderful, like the mountains of New Hampshire.

In 1886 the milltown of Vancouver burned to ashes, and out of the rubble in twenty-five years emerged the city of electric lights, trolleys, lavish mansions, hotels, and the six-story business block of 1911. Yet in Chinatown, not far from the "downtown district," one could see a pig being barbecued on a spit in the street and the Squamish Indians hung their wash to dry on clotheslines stretched between totem poles.

How to fit in, find a place, get a toe hold in this spinning city? This was John's problem, and letters back East to Frost and Margaret were his life lines. His asthma improved, though very likely it was more the breath of freedom than the air itself, the change of spiritual climate from a small New Hampshire village to a city "on the move."

"Letter after letter came from Frost, all about me and my problems," John wrote of this period, though none of these letters was saved. He was hired for his first newspaper job in much the same way Frost was hired at Pinkerton: showing what he could do. He wrote a review of a movie he'd seen in a Chinese theater and showed it to the editor of the Vancouver *News-Advertiser*. John was taken on as a staff reporter covering routine beats at twenty-five dollars a week. Within a few months he had the job well under control, and took on the additional work of writing features for the Vancouver *Sun*. Money in the bank, change in his pockets—in the summer of 1912 he wrote to Margaret, "Meet me half-way on the map!"

It wasn't exactly the kind of wedding a girl dreams about, but to a much-in-love girl of twenty, whose heart had been "given to John at sixteen," there was something wildly romantic about traveling halfway across the continent to meet her lover. They met in Medicine Hat, Alberta (chosen because "we liked the sound of it"), and were married by a stranger without the presence of family or friends. Margaret's wedding gown was a brown wool suit with a hobble skirt, terribly stylish, but dangerous for boarding trains. Nothing was ever said about the romance of a honeymoon trip on the train back to Vancouver.

Margaret's excited qualms about life in the big city (she had never even been to Boston) were short-lived, for the house John had rented for his bride was a frame cottage on a two-acre tract on Lulu Island, across the Fraser river from Vancouver. Tracts and farms surrounded them, neighbors were at a distance, and in New England fashion they immediately set up housekeeping by buying a flock of hens and putting in a strawberry patch. John, as an early-day commuter to the city, rode the electric trolley across the river, picked up his mail at the Eburne Post Office on Sea Island, then continued through the Municipality of Point Grey which then boasted four small but rapidly growing settlements. Mostly what he saw from the electric tram window was a vast field of tree stumps, reminders of the splendid Douglas fir forest of the past, tenaciously holding on by the roots before giving way to suburban developers. New landowners in their haste to build would sometimes live in tents while their property was still being cleared, and there were stories of bears haunting the old forest, wandering among the stumps and blackberry bushes, frightening settlers by breaking into coolers in search of food. Frost caught up the story and tossed it back in a poem:

The Lure of the West

My friends in Vancouver, they write
Of the grand opportunities there:
A man on a neighboring height
Found a new kind of grizzly bear,
Imparting a new kind of scare.
They didn't say how it looked quite,

But calmly went on to declare
That I should have found it by right.

I really don't doubt it a mite:
I can just seem to feel myself dare
To wrap both my arms round the wight
And burying face in its hair.
I don't think the grizzly would care
If I hugged it a little too tight.
Oh wouldn't we make a nice pair?
And wouldn't I make* a nice bite? (*alternative: take)

And all this could happen in sight
Of a busy municipal square!
My friends in Vancouver are bright,
But I'll tell them they'd better beware:
If they sing me much more to that air
I'll take the train west overnight,
And ask them to lend me the fare.
I'm a dangerous man to excite.

Yes, I'll smoke if you'll give me a light,
And yes, you may bring me a chair.
You mustn't suppose this is fright;
I'm just feeling weak—everywhere.

Frost was really tempted to try Vancouver. Even before John and Margaret were married he had talked about it in letters, and John would throw a little kindling on the fire by sending copies of British periodicals, among them, *T.P.'s Weekly* with its columns of literary activity in London. John was finding his place, and in addition to the work on two dailies had become Acting Editor of the Point Grey *Gazette*, a weekly, whose future, like Point Grey itself, was much rosier than its immediate present. Frost's "one year" at Plymouth Normal had increased his reputation as a teacher worth listening to and brought the kind of success that feeds the family and stands well with the neighbors. "But," as he wrote John, "it's the next three or four years, or never," if he were to make his way with his poetry.

Frost's imagination played with the idea of Vancouver, toyed with it, and taking a graphic turn, he sketched a "3-acre Desideratum map," showing on Acre A the successful John, Acting Editor of the Point Grey *Gazette*, ensconced in a "Palatial Residence with Mansard Roof," and on Acre B, his own lean-to sanctuary emitting smoke of activity ("Anabolism, Katabolism"). He included such details as the Bridge of Size and the Footbridge of No Size and, of course, "Bears of a kind not addicted to faring on children over 6 years old, i.e. paying half or whole fare."

"I am willing," he noted at the bottom, "to pay $100 for the front acre. The other ought not to cost so much."

The price of things had to be considered. Money matters loomed large to John and Margaret, the growth of savings representing visible proof of their abilities. Both trembled at the rashness of John's first business venture, for he "loaned" Alec Paton, publisher of the Point Grey *Gazette*, their six hundred dollars in savings to install a new printing press. It was an informal arrangement based on Mr. Paton's firm belief in the future of Point Grey, and John allowed himself to be convinced that poor printing facilities were all that held back the great potential of the *Gazette*. In retrospect, Mr. Paton, who in later years became a leading citizen and Reeve of Point Grey, described his weekly as having "108 subscribers, mostly deadheads or complimentaries, and several columns of advertising which appeared in the paper but not in the cash box." It was a reckless sort of loan, and no doubt increased the young couple's agitation over boom-based living costs which ate up the weekly pay.

It was enough to give Frost thought, and ultimately, so the story goes, Frost tossed a coin to decide whether to move his family to Vancouver and join John and Margaret or go instead to England and "live under thatch," which appealed to Elinor. England was the choice, but even as he set foot on foreign soil in the fall of 1912 with no friends to greet him the threads of chance still linked Frost to John Bartlett. In the *T.P.'s Weekly* John had sent from Vancouver was a column, written by an ex-policeman, describing country walks. It occurred to Frost that here was a man acquainted with both the country and its literary publications. Looking him up, the two men talked over possible places for the Frosts to find housing, and after settling in The Bungalow, Beaconsfield, Buckinghamshire (abbreviated on his letters as "The Bung. Hole, Beaks, Bucks."), Frost asked the same ex-policeman columnist to suggest a publisher for his poems. David Nutt, then, was the first office he walked into with his poems, and the result was a contract for the publication of his first book, *A Boy's Will*.

But these are stories that were told later. The Christmas, 1912, letter, the first of Frost's letters that were saved, ignores facts about themselves as if to minimize the distance between them, which now included an ocean as well as a continent:

"I worry about you when I don't get one letter from you in a month. You never say anything about Alec any more. The new press must be in: has it made no difference in your arrangement with him? It is such matters as that that I am interested in. Is there nothing in the wind? I suppose I am lead to expect kaleidoscopic changes in your fortunes from the way things went when you first struck pay dirt. Not that I want to see you earning any more money—or even as much. I hoped that you would settle down, domesticate, so to speak, on one or other of your two papers and be satisfied with one salary. I infer that you are working at all hours. That may do for a short time. It can't last forever. No matter if it isn't hurting you—and I should like assurance on that head—it is leaving you small leisure for self-improvement (to put it in that ugly utilitarian way). It leaves you small leisure for the good old reading—that's the way I like better to say it. I don't say you must get on. I won't say it. But I do say you must invite your soul. Write something for me, something for someone better than your Vancouver reading public. I venture a hat that you wouldn't have to try very long if you set your John-T. wits to it, to make a place for some of your stuff in some of the weeklies here like T.P's or the new Everyman's. Shape it short. Give it a touch of the color of the far west where the Frazer goes out. Emphasize the social values. Give it a pain, a laugh, a thrill. And there you are. I am at you again as I was in the beginning. I haven't forgotten your Hindu boy. Nothing ever came of him. A pity. But there's better fish you know—The question is who's characters out there? Whom do you run across that you could give a Londoner the feeling of? To the devil with this kind of preaching though unless you are going to take some stock in it. I have half a mind to go to writing up Vancouver myself.

It is altogether painful to me not to hear from you. The long letter Mrs. Frost had from Margaret was some consolation. But we must hear more and more definitely about your health and your satisfaction in your work. Gifts of God is it? Well don't let that scare you into redoubling your efforts to make money when you are working double shifts as it is. Take care of yourself. I'm fond of you in my blundering way. I'm glad your mother doesn't know how fond I am or she might make it a ground for disliking me. One advantage of being so far off is the freedom it confers of saying things in writing I couldn't say to your face. I never had more than one real row with you and that was about Pamir. I was reminded of that today when I was browsing over Asia with Carol. You were the best pupil I ever had and Margaret was the next best. So don't you do a single thing that I don't want you to. I am not expected to say much about the Gifts of God I hope. All I say is don't let them influence you or divert you from your chosen way. Don't let them reduce you to the ranks. Only then will they live and grow up to thank you. Don't you fall into any error about the value of more than enough money at this stage of the game."

If there was a gentle warning in Frost's letter, enough to cast a little coolness on John's glowing optimism that the "Gifts of God" were working in his favor, it was well-timed. Trouble came, unexpectedly and out of John's control, when Margaret took seriously ill with what the doctor diagnosed as an inflamed appendix: Margaret's slim frame, her waist tiny enough to encircle with two hands, left little margin for the devastating effects of prolonged fever and pain. The thought of an operation frightened them both, and they seem to have postponed action, either because there was some doubt in the minds of the doctors or because an operation was looked on as something to try when death was the only alternative.

In the midst of the anxious days of Margaret's illness, quietly and without warning, as a gift, came an unbound copy of *A Boy's Will.* The gift copy did not survive the years, but apparently Frost made up the book himself, trimming the galley proofs he was allowed by his publishers to keep and stitching together the pages for a single volume. With the book he sent a playful presentation dated February 26, 1913:

"About now you are in receipt of my coverless book. Now you are reading it upside down in your excitement. What's the matter? You look pale. I see it all as true to life as in a melodrama. Your wife gathers around the table. The dog gets stepped on—the Indian Runner Dog. And Ruksh the dog utters a fearful cry. No canine cry is that, etc. It curdles the Annie Frazier River. A chair goes over.

'Wait,' you say,
'Wait a minute!'
'Hold on!'

'Give me time!'

'I tell you I can understand this if you give me time and don't hurry me!'

'In fact it isn't that I can't understand it.'

'I can understand it all right.'

'But I can't believe it.'

'It is what I may call the startlingness of the intelligence.'

'Suppose I were to telegraph you from Raymond or some other center where things happen and news is manufactured that Sir Peg a Ramsey had demonstrated on the zylophone that there was more radium than neon and helium than yes than in no.'

'You would be excited, wouldn't you?'

'Come own up. Of course you'd be.'

'It would make all the difference in the world.'

'You'd feature it—you'd call attention to it in a leader.'

'Well it's like that—only—what shall I say?'

'Only more serious, more momentous.'

'So unlike poetry—except Masefield's.'

'If a man has anything he wants to break to us let him use prose—prose is his vehicle.'

'Listen to this—it comes with too great a shock in verse.'

'Get ready:'

'eurt saw thguoht I lla fo erus erom ylnO'

'It is too, too much.'

And so you run on till Mrs. Margaret interposes with a woman's good sense:

'Perhaps if you read it right side up it wouldn't mean so much.'

'It might not mean anything.'

Still I think you will treat the book kindly for my sake. It comes pretty near being the story of five years of my life. In the first poem I went away from people (and college); in the one called A Tuft of Flowers I came back to them actually as well as verbally for I wrote that poem to get my job in Pinkerton as little Tommy Tucker sang for his supper, and Brer Merriam read it for me at a Men's League Banquet in Derry Village because I was too timid to read it myself.

Elinor will be writing to Margaret soon. She has been prevented from doing anything extra by various cares and anxieties of late. Lesley has resprained an ankle she sprained in Derry once and it makes a very bad case. She may be two months off her feet. The specialist in London was grave about it. That is hard on a mother. Lesley had a chance to see her own bones in the x-rays."

For Elinor, who lived closely with illness and suffered penetrating anxieties for her family, the response to Margaret's illness was immediate, with a letter, dated March 18, 1913, off as soon as her worry for Lesley abated:

"We have all felt very badly to know how ill you have been. It is terrible that you should have appendicitis at such a time, and it must have been so hard for John to see you suffering. I think it is much better for you to have the operation now, as soon as you are strong enough for it—perhaps it has already taken place. We seem such a fearful distance apart at such a time as this—two weeks is such a long time to wait for news. I wish very much that I had been there through your trouble. I am not much to lean on, but still my presence might have been a little help, and I am sure that Robert would be a great comfort to John during the time you are in the hospital. I hope with all my heart that you will be much stronger after the operation is over.

Lesley's ankle is getting better, but the doctor thinks she ought not to step on it for two weeks yet. She is very nervous, of course, and it is difficult to make her days pass pleasantly. On pleasant days she sits out in the sunshine for an hour or two. For the last week or two the larks have been back from the South, and quite a flock of them stay in the field that lies over the hedge on one side of our house. I can understand now why the lark is the subject of so much English poetry. Every few minutes one will rise from the ground, as if overcome by emotion, and soar straight up in the air until one can scarcely see him, singing all the while such a sweet, rapturous song, and then let himself straight down again, singing until he reaches the ground. I never heard such a lovely bird song. A great many kinds of flowers are blooming here now. As the weather is much improved, I think we shall have some nice walks when the injured ankle is well again. . . .

Irma wrote this letter to you, intending to copy it with spelling corrected, but as she is so tired, I will send it as it is. I mustn't write any longer today but will write again soon. With a great deal of love and sympathy from your friend Elinor M.F."

"My Dear Margaret,

I am sorry you have been sick, and hope you are better now. I wish you were here and lived next ner as. We would have a great time. England is difrent then america. I we have hedgs. I havent seen a pine tree, we have now wood house, ether, they are all stone and brick and plaster, ours is plaster, one of our trees in front is all blossomed and the leaves ar coming out well on the trees in back. We have a strawberry bed in the back yard. We are digging the ground now, Mama is going to have a radish garden and a lettuce garden, and she is going to have some flowers to, I think papa is going to plant some things, Marjorie and Carol and I are going to have some flowers too. Lesley has a sprained anckle for five weeks, and isn't well yet. She got it in school. It is getting better now we have had the doctor and she has had it bandadged up. I will write when it gets better.

With love from

Irma"

Such words and feelings were a comfort, particularly since both John and Margaret, although always regular in writing home, were careful not to worry the family with their problems. Margaret, still glowing with the newness of being a bride, couldn't bear to write of the loneliness she sometimes felt, with John gone from early morning until late at night, or the disappointment in her Christmas gift from John: two rabbits! "If there was nothing particularly happy to write, why I'd tell about the way the sun made shadows on the mountains," she used to say. Only in writing the Frosts were they able to let go with some of their feelings.

And there was a bigger worry. Unable to recover the "loan" money, but needing money for an operation, John plunged into his work with a fury equal to his anxiety.

Since the *Sun* paid "by the stick," i.e., by the number of column inches appearing in print, he had to produce more copy and get more stories published.

What had Frost written? "Shape it short. . . . who's characters out there?" So the stories came: Biblical Smith, an itinerant preacher of sorts, with a capacity for raising funds, then disappearing quietly; an exposé of Manuel and the Shell Game, a crafty Spaniard with sly eyes and shifty fingers. There were bones discovered in the Vancouver city dump, "thought to be those of prehistoric man!" Most sensational of all was "The Nouvelle Evangeline," star-crossed lovers searching for each other halfway around the world to meet again—in Vancouver—but, alas, too late; death had snatched the loved one across the final barrier. The syndicated press caught the story, and the *Sun* editor wanted more.

John was in a panic. They were lively stories, all right. It was just that they weren't exactly true. Bones had been found, to be sure. Bones were frequently being dug up— Indians, Chinese buried in shallow, temporary graves, to be returned later to the homeland. But they had to be "thought Neanderthal" to rate newspaper space. John's New England conscience pinched, but not as badly as the fear of being found out. Frost was the only one he could tell about this kind of trouble. In early April, 1913, John received his answer:

"My dear dear John:—

Your last letter rather piles on the agony. But we are not going to let it worry us too much. You will be writing in a day or two that Margaret is better or has gone through the operation all right and that Gerry has ceased to press you for further copy on the critturs of your imagination.

But you are terribly overwrought. I see you in a vision as you appeared the day Doe hit you in the eye. If you don't look as wild as that, you feel enough worse to more than make up for it. And yes, I repeat that I didn't get out there where I could perhaps do or say or be a little something to help you over a bad place.

You mustn't fake articles any more. Not even in details. Them's orders. I'll tell you why. It's taking an unfair advantage. Of whom? Of the public? Little I care for them. They would deceive themselves were there no one else to deceive them. Of your follow journalists then? I suspect that they can hold up their end. No it is taking an unfair advantage of the gentlemen who profess fiction. I used to think of it when I faked in a small way for another paper named the Sun which was published in Lawrence Mass. All I had to do was to claim for my yarns the virtue of fact and I had story writers of twice my art and invention skun a mile. I thought of it again when partly for the fun and partly for the lucre I tried my hand at poultry journalism. I wrote up one or two poultrymen as you did Biblical Smith filling in the gaps in my knowledge with dream material. I think I managed fairly well except for the time I spoke of John Hall's geese roosting in the trees. I should have let geese severely alone. It took an artistic letter from John Hall himself (I wrote it for the douce man) to save me from the scandal that started. I had a little right on my side. As a matter of fact John Hall had among others a few Brazilians that sometimes roosted on a pollared willow and even on the chimney and he could honestly say so (if some one would write the letter for him, for he was without clerkly learning.) But I was uncomfortable all the time until I settled back to write out-and-out stories. It had occurred to me previously that some fiction not purporting to be true otherwise than as fiction is true, true to the life of the farm and especially the poultry farm wouldn't derogate from the serious not to say solemn interest of a poultry journal. I succeeded in creating a limited demand for it and was making a very little money when I decided I could make more in Pinkerton. I tell you all this to show you. A little faking in our salad days is none so sinful—a novice naturally takes it as a lark—he can't feel that he has tasted the full flavor of the world the flesh and his grown-up-man's job if he hasn't tried it. But you will soon sicken of it, if you haven't sickened already. Give us a rest about the money you need. I don't want you to get rich too fast.

I speak lightly enough. All the same I shall feel mightily relieved when you write that the danger of your being found out in the Manuel-and-His-Little-Shell Game (Conchita must mean shell) is safely past. What I fear is that someone on Sea Island will rise up to question your authenticity—or the Spanish Consul if there is such a thing on the coast. I should be scared blue if I were in your predicament. No harm in my saying as much at this distance since by the time you hear me you will either have come through safely or have been ridden on a rail out of the Sun office. We will laugh at all these worries some day when we are collaborating on a brisk novel of Vancouver in the days of the land speculation.

Our love to Margaret. Both of you are young and brave and fine and the best stuff ever. Write 'em as short as you please but write oftener. We like to see the paper once in a while.

R.F."

The world didn't come to a crashing end, although they were braced for the shock. The crises passed, on both counts. John was not found out and exposed to public humiliation, and Margaret not only recovered from her appendicitis, if such it was, but became pregnant and her health actually improved with what might have seemed an added complication. But John's fright had been so severe over his newspaper fiction that he missed the obvious point that he was a talented story writer. He never went near fiction again, although his best letters and conversations were about "characters." What the wild swing of the imagination that carried John to a fraudulent extreme did accomplish was to shake him loose from the confinement of routine newspaper work. Although he kept on with the two dailies, using his head instead of his feelings, he branched out with free-lance articles for farm papers. It was the beginning of his life-long career of writing articles.

Regaining his balance, or perhaps emerging from the winter of worries with a new-found feeling of adulthood, John seemed to become aware of the fact that letters from Frost had told him nothing of the how and wherefore of Frost's book of poetry. Although part of John's lack of concern can be attributed to his preoccupation with his own problems, it is also true that even at Pinkerton John never had a doubt that Frost would win recognition simply by presenting his poetry. Apparently the story of finding a publisher had filtered back to them from New

Hampshire. John wanted to hear it first-hand, and had to ask. The reply was written about April 4, 1913:

"The story when pieced together amounted to just this—I don't know whether I have bothered you with it before. I found a publisher for my book in the first office I walked into. The firm pays all expenses of publication which is a very unusual thing in the case of a first book. I am under contract to let the same firm have my next four books if I ever write any more . . .

I have got off the track a little bit. But I think I have told you about the whole story as Silver had it. Where the anxieties come in? Bless you, all that hit my Plymouth friends so hard is just the beginning of a book's career. I am in mortal fear now lest the reviewers should fail to take any notice of it. Such a work isn't sold in the bookstores but through the notices in the papers entirely. It is going the rounds now and it remains to be seen whether it will fall flat or not. Something however it has already done for me in ways too mysterious to go into. It has brought me several interesting friendships which I can tell you about without exciting any jealousy in your breast because you know that I care more for you and your opinion of me (formed when I was fifteenth in command at Pinkerton) than for the opinion of all the rest of them put together. Yeats has asked me to make one of his circle at his Monday Nights when he is in London (and not in Dublin). And he told my dazzling friend Ezra Pound that my book was the best thing that had come out of America for some time. Of course we needn't believe that. I spent the evening with Yeats in his dark-curtained candlelit room last week. We talked about the

Land of Heart's Desire among other things. He is the big man here in poetry of course, though his activity is largely dramatic in late years. I have met Maurice Hewlett within a day or two. Hewlett not very intimately. You know him for his novels. He himself cares only for his poetry. And then there is May Sinclair the author of The Divine Fire etc. etc. I took tea with her yesterday and expect to go there again shortly. She professes to see something unusual in my book. I like that of course because she is known as an expert in new poetry. She is the lady who made the reputation of Vaughn Moody, Torrence and Edwin Arnold Robinson by naming them as the principal poets in the States. And Ezra Pound, the stormy petrel, I must tell you more about him when I have more time. He has found me and sent a fierce article to Chicago denouncing a country that neglects fellows like me. I am afraid he over did it and it may be a mercy all round if it isn't printed. It is likely to be though as he always seems to have his way with the magazine it has gone to. All this ought to be enough to satisfy me for the time being you will think. But dear dear. The boom is not started yet. And then there is the money question. I am going to run short and have to go to the American Consulate for assisted passage home. There is little money ahead. Hewlett was boasting that he had three pounds, his first royalty on a book of poems published four years ago. Gosh."

For some reason a bound copy of Frost's book seemed to excite John more than the coverless copy he'd received six weeks earlier. But then, John was enjoying seeing his own name in print, and was using a personal letterhead announcing John T. Bartlett as "British Columbia Editorial Representative, the Montreal *Weekly Star*," and "Farming subjects, Magazine, Newspaper, and General Publicity Work." The game was becoming real, in the open, with a kind of parental concern for "how it will go." John wrote Frost asking for a trade copy of *A Boy's Will*. Around June 12, 1913, the book was sent along with some suggestions:

"I have to be chary of my favors to get anything out of you. The book goes with this as per your kick of recent date. You are now supposed to order of your own motion and without undue pressure from me not less than fifteen nor more than twenty copies at forty cents (inclusive of post.) the copy. You must do this of the publisher and not of me so as to make it look as if I had taken hold in the far west (why, God only knows). Then you must get me a notice in the most literary of the Vancouver dailies or weeklies. Make it personal if you like, a sort of news item. Like this: Jaunty Bart., the popular and ever censorious fakeer of the Sun staff is in receipt of etc. etc. till you get to 'allow me to sell you a couple' (quoting from Alice). You know the sort of thing. Be sure to say, This is hot stuff. A few choice copies left. Call it a farm product without fear of contradiction. It is inevitable (that's the word) as inevitable as a cabbage or a cucumber (if the cut worms don't get it.) Funny how you and I both go in for farming. I am looked on as someone who has got the poetry of the farm. Can't you ring me into one of your columns in the Montreal Star? In a word do your dambdest and hang the consequences.

46

I am mes enfants
    Living in you more than you can imagine
                R.F."

A Boy's Will, trade copy, arrived with the inscription:
                Outcasts of Lulu Flat
                        from
                    EMF and RF
                Castaways on an Island.

Margaret again received the book in bed, after she had suffered a miscarriage. She'd been chasing the rabbits, never properly penned, and the neighbors had complained about providing tender leaves from their gardens to satisfy the rodents' voracious appetites. Slipping on a grassy slope, the fall prematurely set off labor, and all alone, unable to call for help once she had reached her bed, she waited until John came home, near midnight, to go out again and find a doctor.

Margaret grieved her loss, but privately. She was proud of John's accomplishments, pleased with Frost's book, but felt a failure in what she could do. She wondered, as she used to tell the story, that John didn't seem to understand, though his unreadiness to sympathize may have been simple relief in the termination of a pregnancy a little unwise so quickly after a serious illness.

Elinor, who had lost two babies of her own, knew of the feeling, the effort to find something cheerful in the world outside, and on July 3, 1913, she wrote Margaret a womanly letter:

"It does seem so good to get a letter from you again,

and to know that you are all right. Of course I have reasoned that if anything were at all serious John would let us know about it, but at the same time I have felt certain misgivings about your health, and feared that you might be terribly weak after all your suffering. How fortunate it was that the fine spring weather came to tempt you out of doors. I know exactly how you felt, for the seasons here are much the same as with you, I imagine, and the many weeks of rain and cloudy skies were very depressing. At first, when the pleasant days began to be frequent, I did not have much faith in their going on and on but really we have had as many as six weeks of perfect weather, and England is certainly a charming place in summer. Lots of birds and flowers entirely new to us, you know, and quantities of roses in our own garden. We didn't plant anything. Rob didn't feel in the mood to bother with it, and I haven't had any time what with teaching and sewing and housework. But there are so many fruit trees in the back garden that it is a pleasant spot anyway. The currants and raspberries are just getting ripe. We have had a number of pleasant picnics. We pack a lunch into several different bags, so that we can share the load and tramp off two or three miles through the lanes and paths. We are all feeling ever so well except Lesley. Her ankle is well again, but there is a tendency to flat-foot after the severe strain, and her general health is not very satisfactory. She is growing very fast this year, and somehow she hasn't much strength for anything except growing.

I hope, my dear, that you do not try to do too much housework. I think it is *very necessary* for you to take good care of yourself for several years to come, and you must learn the art of 'letting things go' just as I had to learn it long, long ago. How could I ever have lived through those years when the children were little tots if I had been at all fussy about my housework? Do not try to cook much—wash dishes only *once* a day and use no rooms except kitchen, bedroom and sitting-room, and hire someone to come in and sweep up once in two weeks. That is often enough where there are only two of you. I hope, indeed, that you won't have any more appendicitis, and I almost wish that the old appendix could have been taken out, so that there would be no more danger of it. You and John will have to be very careful, won't you, that you do not become pregnant again for a while. Without doubt, the doctor has cautioned you. You are very young yet. There is plenty of time for a family when you are older and stronger."

[Margaret took such advice coolly. She would never have left a bed unmade or dishes in the sink! And she was very careful not to announce her future pregnancies.]

"I am very glad you and John like Robert's book. Of course I love it very much, and have been somewhat disappointed that the reviewers have not been more enthusiastic. How can they help seeing how exquisitely beautiful some of the poems are, and what an original music there is in most of them? Rob has been altogether discouraged at times, but I suppose we ought to be satisfied for the present to get the book published and a little notice taken of it. Yeats has said to a friend, who repeated the remark to Robert, that it is the best poetry written in America for a long time. If only he would say so publicly, but he won't, he is too taken up with his own greatness.

Robert has made some pleasant acquaintances among the younger writers in London, and several of them have been out to see us. We have become very well acquainted with the family of one of the professors at London University—Professor Gardner. His wife is the author of a Greek grammar and is very kind-hearted, clever and impulsive. There are three children, a daughter, 22 years old, who is an artist, and two younger children, Lesley and Carol's ages. We like them all very much, and they have been very nice to us, but they live on the other side of London, in Surrey, and we cannot see much of them. . . .

I thought it so sweet of John to begin his letter 'Dear Rob'—When we all meet once more, you two must call us by our first names, if it wouldn't seem too strange to you, for, while we are really about twice as old as you are, we don't *feel* at all old.

The children all send their love and thanks for the pretty cards. They are going to write to you soon.

John's letter-head is very imposing, isn't it."

Whatever their personal worries, the women watched their men catching hold in the world. Summer, 1913—the beginnings of fame for Robert Frost, the poet; to John and Margaret, he became "Rob" and remained so for the rest of their lives.

III

Plotting Publicity

Joʜɴ's work on Aggy papers was in part finding the material: training his eye to spot successful ideas for increasing production, be it eggs from chickens or honey from bee hives. Selling was part of the game, as it was part of establishing a reputation as a poet and so with particular interest he was on the lookout for the first notices given *A Boy's Will*. One of the first appeared in *T.P.'s Weekly*, which reviewed Rob's book along with five other new books of poetry. What was said was favorable enough, but the author of the article reviewed the six "in order of merit," placing *A Boy's Will* in fifth place. John, with the indignation of a loyal friend, wrote Frost asking, "Who is this fellow setting himself up as an authority?" The answer was dated "Fourth-of-July, 1913":

"Those initials you quote from T.P.'s belong to a fellow named Buckley and the explanation of Buckley is this that he has recently issued a book with David Nutt, but at his own expense, whereas in my case David Nutt assumed the risks. *And* those other people Buckley reviewed are his personal friends or friends of his friends or if not that simply examples of the kind of wrong horse most fools put their money on. You will be sorry to hear me say so but they are not even craftsmen. Of course there are two ways of using that word the good and the bad one. To be on the safe side it is best to call such dubs mechanics. To be perfectly frank with you I am one of the most notable craftsmen of my time. That will transpire presently. I am possibly the only person going who works on any but a worn out theory (principle I had better say) of versification. You see the great successes in recent poetry have been made on the assumption that the music of words was a matter of harmonised vowels and consonants. Both Swinburne and Tennyson arrived largely at effects in assonation. But they were on the wrong track or at any rate on a short track. They went the length of it. Any one else who goes that way must go after them. And that's where most are going. I alone of English writers have consciously set myself to make music out of what I may call the sound of sense. Now it is possible to have sense without the sound of sense (as in much prose that is supposed to pass muster but makes very dull reading) and the sound of sense without sense (as in Alice in Wonderland which makes anything but

52

dull reading). The best place to get the abstract sound of sense is from voices behind a door that cuts off the words. Ask yourself how these sentences would sound without the words in which they are embodied:

You mean to tell me you can't read?
I said no such thing.
Well read then.
You're not my teacher.
———

He says it's too late
Oh, say!
Damn an Ingersoll watch anyway.
———

One-two-three—go!
No good! Come back—come back.
Haslam go down there and make those kids get out of the track.

Those sounds are summoned by the audile imagination and they must be positive, strong, and definitely and unmistakeably indicated by the context. The reader must be at no loss to give his voice the posture proper to the sentence. The simple declarative sentence used in making a plain statement is one sound. But Lord love ye it mustn't be worked to death. It is against the law of nature that whole poems should be written in it. If they are written they won't be read. The sound of sense, then. You get that. It is the abstract vitality of our speech. It is pure sound—pure form. One who concerns himself with it more than the subject is an artist. But remember we are still talking merely of the raw material of poetry. An ear and an appetite for these sounds of sense is the first qualification of a writer, be it of prose or verse. But if one is to be a poet he must learn to get cadences by skillfully breaking the sounds of sense with all their irregularity of accent across the regular beat of the metre. Verse in which there is nothing but the beat of the metre furnished by the accents of the pollysyllabic words we call doggerel. Verse is not that. Neither is it the sound of sense alone. It is a resultant from those two. There are only two or three metres that are worth anything. We depend for variety on the infinite play of accents in the sound of sense. The high possibility of emotional expression all lets in this mingling of sense-sound and word-accent. A curious thing. And all this has its bearing on your prose me boy. Never if you can help it write down a sentence in which the voice will not know how to posture specially.

That letter head shows how far we have come since we left Pink. Editorial correspondent of the Montreal Star sounds [fine] to me. Gad, we get little mail from you."

John never seems to have worried about "literary" qualities; he had found a kind of writing that he could do, but there were difficulties. Vancouver's boom had gone its distance, and by 1913, although the Board of Trade preferred to use the word "pause," the city was in the midst of a severe economic depression. In a way, the bad times made a ready market for lively articles offering new ideas, but it was a highly competitive matter to place material in shrinking publications. John's own confidence was somewhat restored by recovering two-thirds of the money he had loaned Paton—although the experience had left its mark. He didn't invest in another publication for twenty-five years. His articles were being printed in a widening circle of publications: the *Canadian Countryman*, *The Farmer's Magazine*, and the *Family Herald* and *Weekly Star*. Frost followed John's adventures with gentle amusement at the turn of affairs, as in the letter of summer, 1913:

"I always feel perfectly right for a whole day after I have had a letter from you. You and your tale of Aggy-papers! And do you remember little Dicky Potter, Ben Bolt? You despised him for a farmer once and now look at you writing rabbity poultry articles for a farm journal. We never know. You were studying Greek then; Potter is doubtless teaching it now. Turn, fortune, turn thy wheel and lower the proud.

One of the curious fatalities in our lives is that without collusion we have simultaneously turned our minds to run on rusticity. . . ."

But there were the sweetmeats of success: for John, the extra money, and for Frost, the reviews. Both had left New Hampshire with somewhat less than warm farewells of confidence. They could hardly keep from indulging in thoughts of satisfaction that there would be some Derry people who might be a little uncomfortable knowing things were going well with them, or as Frost put it in a letter written in July, 1913:

"What do you say if we cook up something to bother the enemies we left behind in Derry? It won't take much cooking, but what it does will come on you. You have two of my reviews now. If you haven't I will see that you have others to take their place. One is good for one reason; the other for another. *Pound's* is a little too personal. I don't mind his calling me raw. He is reckoned raw himself and at the same time perhaps the most prominent of the younger poets here. I object chiefly to what he says about the great American editors. Not that I have any love for the two or three he has in mind. But they are better ignored—at any rate they are better not offended. We may want to use them some time. The other I value chiefly for its source, *The English Review* the magazine that found Maesfield and Conrad. The editor himself wrote that particular notice.

I am sending you one more review which you can hold on to for a while. One more still and we shall have the ingredients of our Bouillabaise (sp) assembled. If nothing slips up we will get that in the August number of *The Bookman* (English). The editor has asked me for my photograph and a personal note to accompany the review. I suppose everything depends on whether I look young enough in my photograph to grace the ballet. Why did you wear me out teaching you things you knew already?

Well then in August, say, as soon as you get the Bookman you can begin a little article for Morse-back of The News and Enterprise like this:

Former pupils of R.F. at Pink. may be interested to learn of the success of his first book published in London. A recent number of The Bookman (Eng.) contains etc.— You are not to get the least bit enthusiastic—I know you my child. Keep strictly to the manner of the disinterested reporter. Make the article out of the reviews almost entirely. In mentioning *The English Review* you might mention the fact that it is a leading literary monthly here.

All this is if you have time and inclination. It will necessitate some typewriting. I would copy Ezra Pound's article so as to get rid of the break about the editors. Leave in any derogatory remarks. We like those. I fancy I should leave out the quotation from 'My November Guest' which mangles a poem that needs to be taken as a whole and then quote it as a whole in the *Poetry and Drama* review I am enclosing. You see the scheme is to make *The Bookman* affair the occasion for your article and then drag the rest in by the ears. Say simply 'The following is taken from——' Or if you see some other way to go about it, all right. You might do it in the form of a letter to the News, beginning 'I thought former pupils of RF at Pink etc' and sign yourself J.T.B. Anything to make Mrs. Superior Sheppard and Lil' Art' Reynolds unhappy. (You put these people into my head.) But I suppose I care less about teasing my out-and-out enemies than my half friends like John C. Chase. I told you how I charged John C. forty dollars for the catalogue and when he winced told him that I didn't get it often but when I did I got about that much for my poetry. He never quite got over that. He clipped a cheap joke on poets one day and sent it to me by Miss Bartley so that she would share in my discomfiture. I only stood it tolerably well. I didn't mind it at first as much. I got tired of it."

John didn't answer immediately, being concerned at this time over Margaret who was again pregnant. She was determined, somehow, regardless of her recent miscarriage and in spite of advice to the contrary, to have her baby. She'd made no friends in Vancouver, feeling little in common with neighbors, and John's working hours were such that they rarely took the electric carline to visit his sister Bess. Margaret's loneliness was hard to bear, and she hated her "frailty." This time, nobody was let in on the secret that she was expecting another baby.

c. August 6, 1913

"I have had no word out of you to encourage me to go on with the material for the article you were going to please John C. and Henry's Mother with. You should have three reviews in hand, the one from *Poetry*, the one from *The English Review* and the one from *Poetry and Drama*. I am sending the personal notice from the August English Bookman. You may use them or not in the way I suggested; I shan't care too much if you don't. I know you must be very busy. Consult your own inclination.

None of the articles but should be used with some judgment. This *Bookman* piece for instance makes me out as able to earn a living on a farm with both hands in my Norfolk-jacket pocket. Rats. I should rather you would eliminate that. The word 'stark' in it will do well enough, though it is wide enough of the mark. As things go here in criticism it passes for a term of praise. 'Bizarre' is a way off for A Hundred Collars. But never mind it was kindly meant. And the editor only knew the poem by hear say. On the whole I think the Bookman article needs manipulation as little as any. It is fairly discrete.

Be sure to get rid of the slam at America in the English

Review article; also in the 'Poetry' and 'Poetry and Drama' articles. The remark about the Great American Editors is not quite fair either to the editors or to me. For the rest I leave it to you. Don't let the paragraph in T.P.'s worry you. This getting reviewed for poetry over here is all sorts of a game. The explanation of the T.P.'s reviewer is this. He is my rival for the affections of David Nutt (publisher) and his own little volume of verse hasn't been reviewed at all.

I don't know whether I am a craftsman or not in your sense of the word. Some day I will take time to explain to you in what sense of the word I am one of the few artists writing. I am one of the few who have a theory of their own upon which all their work down to the least accent is done. I expect to do something to the present state of literature in America. That is why I don't want any slaps at my friends at home.

Now don't you do a thing you aren't moved to. Perhaps for some reason you think poorly of the Derry News plan. Would it be better to do it for the Manchester Union?

I am very busy myself for a person whose temperament is so self-obstructive. The next book begins to look large. Though I can't be sure that I will be ready with it this fall. I should like to sell some of it to the magazines first. A few hundred dollars earned that way might save my neck."

Still there was no word from John, no comment on the suggested publicity. The request dangled. Two weeks was the average time for a letter to reach England from

Vancouver. Rob waited two weeks and wrote again on August 30, 1913, from Kingsbarns, Fifeshire:

"To relieve my feelings just a word from Scotland on the funny holiday we are having with the Professor Gardiners. They are a family I got entangled with at the opening of the Poetry Shop in High Holborn last winter. It was not my fault at all. I want you to know one thing: I have thrust myself and book on no one here. I have made my way partly on my merits, mostly on my luck, but I have never forced my way one inch. These Gardiners are the kind that hunt lions and they picked me up cheap as a sort of bargain before I was as yet made. I ought not to draw them too unsympathetically, for they have meant to be kind and I count it to their credit that they have embraced the whole family in their attentions. But, but! There is a string to it all, I find. They are a one-hoss poet and artist themselves and at the present moment they are particularly keen on lions as creatures who may be put under obligations to review them in the papers. Sic ad astra itur in London town. It would make you weep. The Missus Gardiner is the worst. Nothing would satisfy her but we must all pack up and come to Scotland (Firth of Tay) to be near them for two weeks. So we let ourselves be dragged. Now the question is what do we think of their book. Well, I haul off and start to say what I don't think with appropriate sops to my conscience. But such integrity as I have is all literary. I make a poor liar where the worth of books is concerned. I flounder and am lost. Thus much in the historical present. The Gardners don't like me any more. They despise my judgement and resent my tactlessness. But here I am on their hands. They are a gentleman and must carry it off with manners. Himself being an archaeologist (London University) he proposes to entertain us of an afternoon by conducting us to a cave near St. Andrews for a look at an elephant a horse and an ass done by paleolithic man on the walls. These are the first drawings (or cuttings) of cavemen discovered in the British Isles and as Gardner discovered them and the discovery is going to make a stir when it is announced presently naturally we were expected to feel the honour of being taken into what is as yet a profound secret. But, but. Same old hoodoo of my too critical mind. I wanted to see the animals and I saw them. There were many marks on the cave wall, some wavy grooves due to water, some sharp-edged depressions due to the flaking off of the sandstone strata. It would have been strange if some of the marks hadn't accidentally looked like something. The sandstone was so soft and moist that a little rubbing easily made them look more like something. Animals are always the better for rubbing. And think of it—tracery like that and in such a substance assumed to have lasted for ten—twenty thousand years. Why I'd be willing to leave it to the cave men as to whether they had any thing to do with the elephant the horse or the ass. I'll bet the layer of sandstone they are on hasn't been uncovered five hundred years if it has been a hundred. I begin to think I must be some archaeologist myself, I doubted the authenticity of this prehistoric menagerie so easily. The beasts left me cold. I tried to rise to the moment, but the cave was clammy and there were other things, principally the literary literature. Still I have no doubt a rumpus will be raised over Gardner's discovery. Sic ad astra itur in highbrow circles.

Let's see didn't you dig up a Neanderthal man in the Vancouver city dump?

Not a word to your city editor about all this. I am betraying a confidence in consigning it to paper. But damn—

St. Andrews is old enough anyway without the cave drawings. We stood in the town under a tower that has figured in history since the sixth century—St. Regulus' Tower. All round us were the ruins of the great cathedral that John Knox preached his followers into setting on fire during the Reformation. I haven't given you much of this sort of thing. Sounds very travelly.

Dont write to me here. We are only Fifing for a couple of weeks. Pretty little village Kingsbarns—where the king used to store his grain when his capital was in Dunsfermuline town and his Piraeus at Aberdour (read again the ballade of Sir Patrick Spens.) Right forninst us is the Bell Rock Lighthouse which was the Inchcape Bell of Southey's poem. The children like it. I suppose it won't hurt my New Hampshire impressions as I have always been afraid learning a new language might hurt my English style."

Margaret wrote Elinor, but only about things most immediate in her mind. They were leaving the isolated Lulu Island "farm" to move closer to Vancouver proper, selling the chickens and the rabbits. The excitement of the move into a brand-new house she recalled many years later, when she wrote, "whole blocks of houses built for sale stood like lonely wall flowers, the come hither look gradually fading from their fresh, eager faces. At first they had smiled only at 'people with money,' but gradually they would be glad to be caught up for just a short whirl around the floor. Just such a house we rented the year Forrest was born. The forest had but recently covered the land. Across the street lots were partly cleared, and the wood was anybody's for the taking. John would take a cross-cut saw, fitting the logs into fireplace wood. Wooden sidewalks made walking possible during the long rainy season, and one of the pleasantest sounds stored in my memory is the click-click-click of John's shoes as he hurried eagerly home around midnight from his late newspaper assignments. Young ears are sharp, and I could always hear him coming as soon as he turned the corner, and be at the door by the time he reached our walk."

She made no reference to John's work, or the proposed review, or the expected baby. John's apparent coolness in responding to the suggested review began to make Frost uneasy. He wrote from Beaconsfield in October of 1913:

"Never you let that silly business of remembering me to my Derry friends put any strain on your feeling for me. I keep not hearing from you; and I begin to be afraid I have asked you to do more than you could do or wanted to do. Very likely you didn't like the idea of stirring 'em up in our old haunts. I don't know that I blame you. It was just my impulse. You are quite free to beg off in the matter. I trust it is no worse than that. It occurs to me as possible that you may have tried to deliver the article on Birch Street and got a snub for your pains. It would have been through no fault of yours, but you may have been uncomfortable about it all this time. The whole thing is of no importance—utterly. I ought not to give way to thoughts of revenge in the first place. Still there were a few people in Derry who vexed me and one or two who did more than that and I am human enough to want to make them squirm a little before I forgive them.

You are about all I saved from the years I spent in Derry, you and Margaret, and the three children born to us on the farm, and the first book that was mostly written on the farm before I attended school at Pinkerton. I really care not a fig either way for or against any one else I fell in with in my teaching days. I don't want you to grow cold in letter writing. You are to act always on the assumption that we are going to get together again across the meridians. Of course we are. I always think if you would take measures to strike up a correspondence for one of these London papers you would sooner or later land here among the literary people, and with better prospects of staying than I have because you know how to make money. Think it over. I am reminded of you every time I see a special article from British Columbia.

You mustn't take me too seriously if I now proceed to brag a bit about my exploits as a poet. There is one qualifying fact always to bear in mind: there is a kind of success called 'of esteem' and it butters no parsnips. It means a success with the critical few who are supposed to know. But really to arrive where I can stand on my legs as a poet and nothing else I must get outside that circle to the general reader who buys books in their thousands. I may not be able to do that. I believe in doing it—don't you doubt me there. I want to be a poet for all sorts and kinds. I could never make a merit of being caviare to the crowd the way my quasi-friend Pound does. I want to reach out, and would if it were a thing I could do by taking thought. So much by way of depreciation before I begin. Now for it, a little of it.

I suppose I arrived in a sense the other day when Laurence Binyon asked me to lunch with Robert Bridges the Laureat. It meant this much: Binyon had decided that my book was one of the few and he was good enough to want me to have my chance with the Chief. So I took it. That is the best sounding thing I have to tell. I don't know that it pleased me any more than to find Trevelyan, a man who is known as a patron of art, with my book in his pocket. He had bought it on the recommendation of somebody who is supposed to know all about poetry. I am sure that it pleased me less than the friendly attentions I have had from Wilfred Gibson and Lascelles Abercrombie. These fellows you can know if you can get hold of either Q's Oxford Book of Victorian Verse or The Georgian Anthology. They are something more than my casual acquaintances. If or when we can get rid of this house I am going down into Gloucester to live near them. The second book is what has drawn them to me. Some of the manuscript has been passed around and they have seen it.

I think that's all except that Mrs. Nutt in her devotion to my cause has already announced the second book without waiting for me to say the word. So the anxiety of finding a publisher is off my mind. As the boys say here, It is success enough if your first book does well enough to get you a publisher for the second. The book should be out in February. You shall have some of it before then if you write me a decent letter and give me your new address. Gone out of the rabbit business, hey? Ain't working the land? Easier to write about it? Think I don't understand?

You and Margaret ought to see how few pieces of furniture we keep house with. It is cosy enough, but it would be a lesson to you in plain living. I would give anything if you could drop in on us."

John's slowness in typing out the review of *A Boy's Will*—for Frost had very nearly set it all down for him— may have easily been just the press of his own affairs: helping Margaret when possible, house-hunting and moving, his articles—all in addition to the double newspaper job. Beginning again were John's recurrent asthma attacks, with a strong tendency to try to ignore the wheezing as something he couldn't afford to have bothering him with a baby coming.

Or he may have held off writing until just the right review came into his hands, the enthusiastic and detailed praise that appeared in the *Academy* in September. John took this, instead of Rob's suggested *Bookman* review, for his lead, using the excerpts Frost had outlined, but making one exception. He included the derogatory remarks about American poetry in *The English Review* quotation. John couldn't resist wanting to show off his friend. But he did make the mistake of thinking that *Poetry*, the magazine in which Pound's review appeared, was a London publication. He always thought, though he never advertised the distinction, that he wrote the first account of Frost's success published by an American paper. The Derry *News* printed the following account on November 1913:

Robert Frost Gaining a Reputation As
Writer of Choice Poems.

Former pupils of Robert Frost at Pinkerton will be interested to learn of the success of his first book, "A Boy's Will," published from the press of David Nutt, London, in the spring. This little book, a collection of poems the local color of which is taken from the Derry and Windham districts, earned for its writer an immediate and warm welcome to London literary circles. The reviewers have been pleasingly complimentary. He is declared a "find," and his poetry "the best to come out of America for years." To those at Pinkerton who came closely in touch with Mr. Frost's delightful personality, and especially those to whom a knowledge of his literary work and ambitions was permitted, his success is peculiarly gratifying. Quite a number of poems in "A Boy's Will" were written while the author was at Pinkerton, and one of them, "A Late Walk," was published in the Critic.

Living with his family at Beaconsfield, a pretty suburb of London, the home of Gilbert K. Chesterton and other literary celebrities, Mr. Frost is, in a distinctly literary atmosphere, devoting himself to his chosen work. He has prepared for publication this fall a second volume of verse, "Farm Servants and Other People," the material for which was gathered while farming on the Turnpike in Windham. The publisher is again David Nutt, who has closed a contract with Mr. Frost for all of his work.

Several reviews and extracts from reviews will convey an idea of the reputation to which this former Pinkerton teacher has attained. The poems quoted will of themselves explain his quick rise to popularity. "We wish we could fitly express the difference which marks off 'A Boy's Will' from all the other books here noticed," said *The Academy*, a London literary weekly in its issue of September 20. "Perhaps it is best hinted by stating that the poems combine, with a rare sufficiency the essential qualities of inevitability and surprise. We have read every line with that amazement and delight which are too seldom evoked by books of modern verse. Without need of qualification or a trimming of epithets, it is undoubtedly the work of a true poet. We do not need to be told that the poet is a young man: the dew and the ecstasy—the audacity, too—of pristine vision are here. At the same time, it is extraordinarily free from a young poet's extravagances; there is no obtrusion of self-consciousness, no labored painting of lilies, nothing of the plunge and strain after superthings. Neither does it belong to any modern school, nor go in harness to any new and twisted theory of art. It is so simple, lucid and experimental, that, reading a poem, one can see clearly with the poet's own swift eyes, and follow the trail of his glancing thought. One feels that this man has seen and felt: seen with a revelatory, a creative vision: felt personally and intensely; and he simply writes down, without confusion or affectation, the results thereof. Rarely today is it our fortune to fall in with a poet expressing himself in so clear a vein. No one who really cares for poetry should miss this little book. There is scarcely a poem of them all but will reward with a thrill, and many of them will yield much more. If we must select, The Trial by Existence must be mentioned for power of imagination; Pan With Us for spirit and sufficiency and for its beautifully clean finish; October for its neat skilful handling; and Storm Fear for its stark articulation in which every word tells. This last is well worthy of full quotation:—

> When the wind works against us in the dark,
> And pelts with snow
> The lower chamber window on the east,
> And whispers with a sort of stifled bark,
> The beast,

"Come out! Come out!"—
It costs no inward struggle not to go,
Ah, no!
I count our strength,
Two and a child,
Those of us not asleep subdued to mark
How the cold creeps as the fire dies at length—
How drifts are piled
Dooryard and road ungraded,
Till even the comforting barn grows far away
Whether 'tis in us to arise with day
And save ourselves unaided.

"We have not the slightest idea who Mr. Robert Frost may be, but we welcome him unhesitatingly to the ranks of the poets born, and are convinced that if this is a true sample of his parts he should presently give us work far worthier of honor than much which passes for front-rank poetry at the present time."

The *English Review*, the magazine that "found" Masefield and Conrad, published the following appreciation, from the pen of its editor:—

"It does one good to glance awhile into the simple woodland philosophy of Mr. Frost. Nowhere on earth, we fancy, is there more outrageous nonsense printed under the name of poetry than in America and our author, we are told, is an American. All the more credit to him for breaking away from this tradition—if such it can be called—and giving us not derivative, hypersensuous drivel, but an image of things really heard and seen. There is wild, racy flavor in his poems; they sound that inevitable response to nature which is the hall-mark of true lyric feeling."

In the August number of *The Bookman* (Eng.) there appeared a photograph of Mr. Frost and a sketch of his life . . . . "After his marriage," it said in part, "he cut himself off from his other belongings, and for several years lived with his wife and children on a New Hampshire farm. Much of his first volume was written in those days and reveals his love of nature and of the loneliness of the woods and fields, touches in pictures of the every day life that lay about him, and is filled with musings on the mysteries of existence, his dreams of what lies behind him, and his hopes of the future. His verse has a strong individual note, and is marked by an unaffected simplicity and a stark directness of utterance that breathes of austere living and the open air."

"The intrinsic merits of the poems are great, despite faults of diction here and there, occasional inversions, and lapses where he has not been strong enough to hear his own simplicity of utterance," said *Poetry and Drama*, London. "It is this simplicity which is the great charm of the book and it is simplicity which proceeds from a candid heart:

My November Guest

My Sorrows when she's here with me,
   Thinks these dark days of autumn rain
Are beautiful as days can be;
She loves the bare, the withered tree;
   She walks the sodden pasture lane.

Her pleasure will not let me stay.
   She talks and I am fain to list:
She's glad the birds are gone away
She's glad her simple worsted grey
   Is silver now with clinging mist.

The desolate, deserted trees,
   The faded earth, the heavy sky,
The beauties she so truly sees,
She thinks I have no eye for these,
   And vexes me for reason why.

Not yesterday I learned to know
The love of bare November days
Before the coming of the snow,
But it were vain to tell her so,
And they are better for her praise.

"Other poems almost or quite as perfect as the one above are: A Late Walk, To the Thawing Wind, Mowing, Going for Water, Reluctance. Each poem is the complete expression of one mood, one emotion, one idea. I have tried to find in these poems what is most characteristic of Mr. Frost's poetry; and I think it is this: direct observation of the object and immediate correlation with the emotion—spontaneity, subtlety in the evocation of moods, humour, and ear for silences. But behind all is the heart and life of a man."

One more review and we are done. It appeared in *Poetry,* also a London publication, and particular interest attaches to it because its author was an American who, like Mr. Frost, is now living in England. Ezra Pound is a Chicagoan, already looked upon as one of the most prominent of the younger poets in Great Britain. "There is another personality in the realm of verse," he wrote, "another American found on this side of the water by an English publisher long known as a lover of good letters. David Nutt publishes at his own expense 'A Boy's Will', by Robert Frost. Mr. Frost's book is a little raw, and has in it a number of infelicities; underneath them it has the tang of the New Hampshire woods, and it has just this utter sincerity. It is not post-Miltonic or post-Swinburnian or post-Kiplonian. This man has the good sense to speak naturally and to paint the thing as he sees it, and to do this is a very different thing from gunning about for the circumplectious polysyllable. It is almost on this account that it is a difficult book to quote from. . . .

"I remember that I was once canoeing and thirsty and I put in to a shanty for water and found a man there who had no water and gave me cold coffee instead. And he didn't understand it, he was from a minor city and he just set there watchin' the river, and didn't seem to want to go back, and didn't much care for anything else. And so I presume he entered into Anunda. And I remember Joseph Campbell telling me of meeting a man in a desolate waste of bogs, and he said to him, 'It's rather dull here'; and the man said, 'Faith, ye can sit on a midden and dream stars.'

"And that is the essence of folk poetry with distinction between America and Ireland. And Frost's book reminded me of these things . . . One reads the book for the 'tone,' which is homely, by intent, and pleasing, never doubting that it comes direct from his life, and that no two lives are the same.

"He has now and then such a swift and bold expression as
    " 'The whimper of hawks beside the sun.'

"He has now and then a beautiful simile well used, but he is for the most part as simple as the lines in the poem of mowing—

There was never a sound beside the wood but one,
  And that was my long scythe whispering to the ground.
My long scythe whispered and left the hay to make.

"He is without sham and without affectation."

J.T.B.

Vancouver, B.C.

The article was reprinted in The Plymouth *Normal School Prospect* with the note that "the writer, one of Mr. Frost's former pupils, is now a succesful journalist in Vancouver. Mr. Frost was a teacher in Plymouth Normal School two years ago." Margaret sent a copy to

Rob along with a letter which he answered immediately on December 8, 1913.

"It was the greatest relief when Margaret's letter came and set my mind at rest. I write so hard when I do write that in the intervals of excitement I simply slump an easy prey to doubts and fears.

In the same mail with Margaret's letter came a copy of *The Plymouth Normal School Prospect* with a reproduction of the whole of what you did for me in *The News*. You exercised the proper discretion. If I have a fault to find it is with the rosy picture you painted of our life in the pretty London suburb inextricably involved in the literary society of the great. But the exaggeration does your heart credit and it wont hurt me as much as it will some people in Derry. (Christ forgive me the sin of vengefulness: from this hour forth I will have no more of it. Perhaps I only say so because for the moment I am sated.) We *could* go among the great (in our humble way—we are far from important yet) but at the same time we can't. Our means forbid. Wander not from the point I keep making that we are playing a rather desperate game with our little wealth. The poets here are of three kinds—the poor rats in one room and a suit of clothes with no family to take care of and much too cunning to be caught in that trap, the gentlemanly minors with a graceful weakness for verse and by common consent quite rich enough to indulge it and the few like Masefield who arrive at one jump. I am like none of these. I must make my way very slowly: such is my doom I am afraid. There will be little money return directly from my

73

poetry—at least for the present. Indirectly if I am clever enough and strong enough I may get some part of a living out of it by following it up with commercial prose. Mrs. Nutt looks for that. The paralizing thought is that I was always a poor hand to do what I had to do: I write bad stuff under pressure. So you see I am no stranger to worry. All is not beer and skittles that wears the look at six thousand miles.

I think Silver may have written the few words of introduction to your article in *The Prospect*. He spoke of you as a 'distinguished journalist of Vancouver' and formerly a pupil of mine, at Derry. Very nice of him all round. I didn't know how he would relish my glorification. I never know how to take him, as friend or enemy. I used to notice he believed what I said about people. I stood in with him that much. I never said you were even better than you showed in school without seeing sooner or later its effect on him. Now it is working the other way. I helped establish your reputation with him and now you are increasing mine with him. We must both walk up and simultaneously ask a big favor of him when he gets to be king of New Hampshire.

I don't know how much of the new book to send at once. It will be more fun to throw it to you in pieces. Here are four or five to start with. *Poetry and Drama* for this month will have two more: *Poetry* at an early date, one and perhaps two. I'll see that you get those. *Poetry and Drama*, a quarterly, costs so much it will have to be my Christmas present to you this year. I am literally and disgustingly busted. The book will be called 'North of Boston'. . . .

In 'North of Boston' you are to see me performing in

a language absolutely unliterary. What I would like is to get so I would never use a word or combination of words that I hadn't heard used in running speech. I bar words and expressions I have merely seen. You do it on your ear. Of course I allow expressions I make myself. War on cliches."

Rob's Christmas present, appropriately enough, was a sample of himself as critic. The copy of *Poetry and Drama*, kept through the years, though now yellow with age and mouse-eaten on some of the margins, contains notations by Frost on nearly all the poems; the exceptions: "The Fear" and "A Hundred Collars," which bear no comments by the author.

Beside "Children of Love" by Harold Monro, Rob wrote: "The gloomy spirit that edits this. No one can laugh when he is looking. His taste in literature is first for the theological and after that for anything that has the bits of sin. He got up a penny sheet of Blake to sell in the slums and you ought to have seen the risky selections he made. But dear me everybody is writing with one foot in the red-light district."

Opposite Rupert Brooke's "He Wonders Whether to Praise or to Blame Her," is the comment: "We know this hardly treated girl, oh very well. Her beauty is her red hair. Her cleverness is in painting. She has a picture in the New England Exhibition. Her mother has written a volume of verse in which he gets his. Very funny. No one will die." And in the margin beside "The Way that Lovers Use," simply: "Wow!"

Robert Bridges, Thomas Hardy, Walter de la Mare,

Frances Cornford; each of their poems bears a Frostian comment.

Of W.H. Davies' "The Bird of Paradise" Frost says: "Davies is lovely; tramped America till he lost a leg under a freight car. Came home and sold his own ballads on penny sheets till they gave him a pension to take him off the streets. Has done some good things in unconscious art. Said he to me, 'I remember you were there the other night. I spoke to you didn't I? But I was awful. After you went I went out of the restaurant a minute for one more drink and I never found my way back.' "

John Alford, about whose poetry Frost had commented, "This boy has taken a dislike to me on account of a review in which he suffered in comparison with me. Here we get down to someone who just can't write poetry," wrote an article in which he attempted to review sixteen volumes of American poetry in four pages. The top of the page contains Alford's statement: "Now it is just as well to state at the beginning that I can find no support to a belief that there is any such thing as American poetry; just as an examination of the Metropolitan Museum of New York finally destroyed my idea that there was any such thing as American art." Frost wrote: "This is what makes it impossible that I should live long under a criss-cross flag. Me for the three colors the blue-bird wears"; and on the bottom margin: "This cub doesn't know how to find his way around American writers. No one he mentions is thought anything of on the other side —no one of recent date. Emerson is so American, so original, especially in form. I'll bet you five he couldn't read him if he tried.

'Whitman and Poe ad stomachache.' "

Alford gave such poets as Cale Young Rice, Clinton Scollard, and Charles M. Lewis their due, a judgment Frost shared: "Not that I weep for these." And on a remark about "cosmicality" in American poetry: "This is true. But one gets tired of hearing it."

Frost explained the remark that "Mr. Pound is a unique phenomenon, for he has succeeded in being an American, a man of culture, and a poet, all at the same time." His note read: "The magazine has had a row with Ezra. This is the olive branch. Monro needs him in his business."

Poet among poets on foreign soil, he remained unmistakably American, unmistakably Frost in his Christmas gift, 1913.

IV

Return to New Hampshire, 1915-1917

THE second winter in Vancouver should have been easier, with Margaret a good deal happier as she made preparations for the baby due in March. For John there was the settled routine of writing for the dailies, the finding of new markets for his free-lance articles. But a restlessness of spirit gnawed at him. He began to feel the monotony of writing daily obituaries, more depressing than the subject. His initial optimism and burst of energy had spent itself, much as Vancouver had burst the bubble of expansion; instead of adventure and pioneering, the whole structure of Vancouver, and his own life, seemed built on dreams and schemes, with fitful successes but no solid base and no satisfactory outlet for his ambitions. He was too impatient for a long-range view, too much in a hurry to feel a deep attachment to Vancouver. The feelings were hard to express, uncertainties difficult to write, but Rob caught the tone. In a letter dated February 22, 1914, he wrote:

"I consent not to guess, but I insist on knowing. And I don't intend to wait too many 'moons of Marriage' either.

I feel as if I were losing track of you you write so seldom and so meagrely not to say mysteriously. The facts of your case as I have them at date are these: Some thing is going to happen to you in not more than nine months that you refuse to tell me about till it happens.

You have lost a lot of money by Alex Paton, but you expect to get 250 dollars out of him. I shall feel better when I hear that you have it.

You are still earning something a week from The Sun and something a week from several other papers. At least you haven't told me that you aren't.

I'm not supposed to know it if you are not writing for an agricultural paper or two and one monthly magazine.

You have friends in that bad country, one of them a highly educated journalist who knows so much more about poetry than you that you let him tell you what is good poetry and what isn't.

The District of Columbia is bad country in every way, physically socially and financially.

You don't mind making me tremble a little (as much as you can) for your security away off there at your age and with a wife to support.

You are dissatisfied with journalism as she is in Vanc. (I wonder if the Editor of The World that Marie Dowd whipped isn't dissatisfied with it too? Was he someone you wanted whipped?)

You don't like your own stuff. You are tired of it. It seems to you to come the same way all the time as it naturally would on the same monotonous subject.

You are fairly well, though not perfectly free from asthma. You would probably be as sick as you used to be if you weren't so much happier than you used to be. I wonder if you think it would kill you to go back to New England. It wouldn't break your heart anyway, would it?

Some of these informations I am indebted to Margaret for. I think I have set down all I know or am warranted in inferring.

I don't mind your being tired of your own stuff. Isis got tired of the millions of men and sought the millions of the Gods but in the end she got tired of the millions of the gods and sought the millions of the spirit. Much virtue in getting tired of your work if you are free enough in body or mind either to go away from it or to convert it into something different or better.

I set a good deal of store by the magazine work you are doing or going to do. That is your way out of bondage. You can—must write better for a magazine than there is any inducement to do for a daily.

My notion is that your work is coming on. Your style tightens up. What you will have to guard against is the lingo of the newspaper, words that nobody but a journalist uses, and worse still, phrases. John Cournos who learned his trade on the Philadelphia Record, where he went by the nickname of Gorky, has come over here to write short stories. He is thirty. His worst enemy is going to be his habit of saying cuticle for skin.

I really liked what you wrote about me. Your sentences go their distance, straight and sure and they relay each other well. You always had ideas and apprehended ideas. You mustn't lose that merit. You must find some way to show people that you have initiative and judgement. You must 'get up' new things as new even as a brand new department for some paper.

But as I was about to say, I am sure your style improves. Let me see some of the more important things you do. I'll traverse them line by line with a pencil if you will let me. Some of my criticism may be wrong but it will stir you up. It wont hurt you and you won't let it offend you.

You can know and you are going to know as much about poetry and any other form of literature as anybody. You know a good deal more now than you think you do, as would soon transpire if you and I were where we could protract talk.

I want to write down here two or three cardinal principles that I wish you would think over and turn over now and again till we *can* protract talk.

I give you a new definition of a sentence:

A sentence is a sound in itself on which other sounds called words may be strung.

You may string words together without a sentence-sound to string them on just as you may tie clothes together by the sleeves and stretch them without a clothes line between two trees, but—it is bad for the clothes.

The number of words you may string on one sentence-sound is not fixed but there is always danger of over loading.

The sentence-sounds are very definite entities. (This is no literary mysticism I am preaching.) They are as definite as words. It is not impossible that they could be collected in a book though I don't at present see on what system they would be catalogued.

They are apprehended by the ear. They are gathered by the ear from the vernacular and brought into books. Many of them are already familiar to us in books. I think no writer invents them. The most original writer only catches them fresh from talk, where they grow spontaneously.

A man is all a writer if *all* his words are strung on definite recognizable sentence sounds. The voice of the imagination, the speaking voice must know certainly how to behave how to posture in every sentence he offers.

A man is a marked writer if his words are largely strung on the more striking sentence sounds.

A word about recognition: In literature it is our business to give people the thing that will make them say, 'Oh yes I know what you mean.' It is never to tell them something they don't know, but something they know and hadn't thought of saying. It must be something they recognize.

A Patch of Old Snow

In the corner of the wall where the bushes haven't been trimmed, there is a patch of old snow like a blow-away newspaper that has come to rest there. And it is dirty as with the print and news of a day I have forgotten, if I ever read it.

Now that is no good except for what I may call certain

points of recognition in it: patch of old snow in a corner of the wall,—you know what that is. You know what a blow-away newspaper is. You know the curious dirt on old snow and last of all you know how easily you forget what you read in papers.

Now for the sentence sounds. We will look for the marked ones because they are easiest to discuss. The first sentence sound will do but it is merely ordinary and bookish: it is entirely subordinate in interest to the meaning of the words strung on it. But half the effectiveness of the second sentence is in the very special tone with which you must say—news of a day I have forgotten—if I ever read it. You must be able to say Oh yes one knows how that goes. (There is some adjective to describe the intonation or cadence, but I won't hunt for it.)

One of the least successful of the poems in my book is almost saved by a final striking sentence-sound (Asking for Roses.)

Not caring so very much *what* she supposes.

Take My November Guest. Did you know at once how we say such sentences as these when we talk?

She thinks I have no eye for these.
_____

Not yesterday I learned etc.
_____

But it were vain to tell her so
_____

Get away from the sing-song. You must hear and recognize in the last line the sentence sound that supports, No use in telling him so.

Let's have some examples pell-mell in prose and verse because I don't want you to think I am setting up as an authority on verse alone.

My father used to say—
You're a liar!
If a hen and a half lay an egg and a half etc.
A long long time ago—
Put it there, old man! (Offering your hand)
I aint a going [to] hurt you, so you neednt be scared.

Suppose Henry Horne says something offensive to a young lady named Rita when her brother Charles is by to protect her. Can you hear the two different tones in which she says their respective names. "Henry Horne! Charles! I can hear it better than I can say it. And by oral practice I get further and further away from it.

Never you say a thing like that to a man!
And such they are and such they will be found
Well I swan!
Unless I'm greatly mistaken——
Hence with denial vain and coy excuse
A soldier and afraid! (afeared)
Come, child, come home.
The thing for me to do is to get right out of here
     while I am able.
No fool like an old fool.

It is so and not otherwise that we get the variety that makes it fun to write and read. *The ear does it.* The ear is the only true writer and the only true reader. I have known people who could read without hearing the sentence sounds and they were the fastest readers. Eye readers we call them. They can get the meaning by glances. But they are bad readers because they miss the best part of what a good writer puts into his work.

Remember that the sentence sound often says more than the words. It may even as in irony convey a meaning opposite to the words.

I wouldn't be writing all this if I didn't think it the most important thing I know. I write it partly for my own benefit, to clarify my ideas for an essay or two I am going to write some fine day (not far distant.)

To judge a poem or piece of prose you go the same way to work—apply the one test—greatest test. You listen for the sentence sounds. If you find some of those not bookish, caught fresh from the mouths of people, some of them striking, all of them definite and recognizable, so recognizable that with a little trouble you can place them and even name them, you know you have found a writer.

Before I ring off you may want to hear the facts in the case of us.

We are still in Beaconsfield but trying hard to get rid of our house six months before our lease is out in order to get away into Gloucester with Wilfrid Gibson and Lasselles Abercrombie (see Victorian anthology for both of them).

Book II, North of Boston, should be out now. The publisher is dilatory. I shall have another book done (out and out plays this time) before she gets Book II out. This is rough on me because I feel that now is the time to strike while there is a certain interest in me for what I have done.

I expect to be roasted more for Book III than for Book II—if for no other reason, because the fact is out that I am an American. That nasty review by Alford in the magazine I sent shows you how they feel toward us here. He begins by saying he can't get hold of enough books to find out whether we have any literature or not and then he proceeds to say we have none. I am sure he will lay for me somewhere. And there are others who have me marked.

J.C. Smith (editor of an edition of Shakespeare and several other classics for the Oxford library) will give an evening to a new American poet named Me before an Edinburgh literary society in March.

Poetry (Chicago) printed in Feb the thing I call The Code. Did I send it to you? If I didn't, you may want to look it up. It may be in the library.

No money comes in of course yet. I won't make much from poetry—I suppose you know that. I talk about prose but as long as I can put off writing pot boilers I shall. It seems to me as I look at it now I had much rather farm than write for money.

We plan to go home in September of 1915. I don't know where I shall settle. You may be coming back to New England some time. Somehow we must plan to be together.

The children all keep well but as they have found the schools impossible here they come pretty heavily on Elinor. She has not been at all well this year. I may have to give up my wilder schemes and turn to money making for the family. Not that I am ever asked to. On the contrary.

I wonder if there is anything more you are as anxious to hear as I am anxious to hear more about you.

Our love to you both. And may God amend my spelling."

With the birth of baby Forrest, named for Margaret's favorite brother, John and Margaret drew their cares closer and held them more tightly. For all the joy in the baby's birth, "the happiest day we have ever known," there was a kind of wistfulness expressed by Margaret in a letter to a school chum. "We wish we might show him to all our folks and friends in the east, but I'm sure I don't know when we will ever see the east again."

There was a falling off in letter writing, with few letters received, or saved, from Frost. John's health was slipping and the asthma attacks could no longer be ignored. When the baby was five months old, on the advice of a doctor to give up newspaper work for a while and seek a higher climate, John let go of the enervating dailies. He made arrangements to write for a newly planned agricultural page in the Vancouver *Province*, and had the stimulus of the *Canadian Countryman*, the *Farmer's Magazine*, and other periodicals for articles from the agriculturally rich Okanagan Valley. The plans were carefully made, so using nearly all their savings, they boarded the train for Okanagan Landing, "the end of the line."

It was early August, 1914, and while they were on the train England declared war against Germany. Just what this meant was not immediately apparent; the more immediate catastrophe was the Oliver No. 5 typewriter which somehow arrived at their destination with the type bars crushed. All copy sent from Okanagan was painstakingly written in Margaret's small, even handwriting.

The effect of the war was distastrous to their plans. The *Province* had to give up the proposed farm page; periodicals found themselves without paper, and without income to pay for editorial material. One editor wrote, "We'll give you subscriptions for each article you write. You can sell the subscriptions and keep the money." But John was no subscription salesman.

Still, there was a coziness about their life in Okanagan. For Margaret, it was having her husband home after the months in Vancouver with John gone from early morning until nearly midnight. There was a primitive satisfaction in spearing kickaninnies (small salmon) in the creek and gathering pails of mushrooms from the orchards to provide food for the table. They tried a new baby food, and Forrest, who hadn't been gaining as well as he should, began to grow husky. Such were John's memories of the Okanagan. And Margaret, many years later when her grandchildren began arriving, recalled those few months:

"Our home was a shack, built for transient orchard workers, perched a little way up a barren hill between the settlement's two grocery stores. At dusk that fall and winter I would go down to one of these stores to buy our meager stock of groceries and visit for a half hour or so with Marguerite, the proprietor's unmarried daughter—my only connection with the outside world.

"It would be dark when I would start back up the hill, and the little house would look lonely and forsaken, and suddenly I, too, would feel alone, defeated, lonely. But the moment I opened the door, joy leaped in my heart. John sat before the small, heat-reddened cookstove, our white-nightied Baby Forrest face down across his knees. The stove had a small firebox and the firewood was long, so long the door of the firebox was dropped to admit the too-long sticks which John pushed, as they burned, farther into the box. Thus, light of the flames leaping from the crackling wood escaped and danced in a merry pattern on the rough-planed wall, on the springless, clumsily nailed together bed, the bench-like chairs, the uneven table, the box cupboard on the wall, softening their shapes and tinting with mellow orange. A full kettle sang on the stove, and often a savory stew bubbled. John rocked rhythmically, gazing into the fire, dreaming, and patting the soft baby's back in time to the motion of the chair. The baby cooed and kicked, plucking long, black horsehairs from a hole in the bottom of the red plush-covered seat of the only factory made chair in the room.

"A shack, a sparsely furnished room, scarcely more than pennies in the pocket . . . yet in one breath, one glance, I knew all the warmth and wealth and wonder of living a woman could ever know."

But such a precarious living couldn't last. Creature comforts can be ignored in good weather. In winter, they can hardly be denied. The outlet for free-lance farming articles was minimal, with no hope of change; the war simply went on. John's breath rattled in his lungs just as the wind whistled and shook the creaky boards of the house. He would lie down at night, exhausted, drop off to sleep, and awaken gasping for breath. He would prop himself up on pillows, or sometimes wrap up in a blanket and sit upright in a chair all night to relieve the weight he felt on his chest. Sleep, when it finally came, would last well into the morning, a pattern he followed the rest of his life, seldom getting up before ten whether suffering from asthma or not. In Okanagan there was no relief. When Margaret discovered she was pregnant again ("and we were so careful!") the risks of staying were too great. They packed their few belongings and in early spring of 1915 returned to New Hampshire, Frost and his family having come home from England only a month or two earlier.

Frost's homecoming was the opening up of a new kind of life. He was a Poet, which made a difference on the demands for his time, but he sought out John as soon as possible. Not hearing from John after his first visit, Frost wrote around the twentieth of April, 1915:

"There seems nothing to talk about on my side but the winning subject of the fortunes of my book. Some day there will be an end of that. You can't wonder that it is a good deal on my mind with a review appearing every few days and letters coming in from all quarters. I wish I could describe the state I have been thrown into. I suppose you could call it one of pleasurable scorn when it is not one of scornful scorn. The thought that gets me is that at magazine rates there is about a thousand dollars worth of poetry in N.O.B. that I might have had last winter if the people who love me now had loved me then. Never you doubt that I gave them the chance to love me. What, you ask, has come over them to change their opinion of me? And the answer is What?—Doubtless you saw my countenance displayed in The Herald one day. The Transcript will [do] me next. The literary editor of The Chicago Post writes to say that I may look for two columns of loving kindness in The Post in a day or two. It is not just naught—say what you will. One likes best to write poetry and one knew that he did that before one got even one reputation. Still one can't pretend not to like to win the game. One can't help thinking a little of Number One.

I couldn't or wouldn't go into all this with anyone else as I am inclined to go into it with you. I feel as if it couldn't hurt you, (You are no fool) and may even do you some good. I want you to see young what a thing it is. Not that I'm on exhibition as a very terrible example—more as an amusing and edifying example. I don't say that any one should actually be warned to avoid my mistakes. But there they are for anyone to avoid who likes to and knows how to.

You alone of my American friends haven't wished me a pot of money out of my poetry. Is it because you are too wise or because you have too good taste or because you are too unworldly to have thought of it. And yet I need money as I suspect you may yourself.

Are you saving your talk of plans for when I am South again in a week or two? Say any thing you choose that comes into your head without fear of actual hurt to me. Write it [down] It will give me something to think of."

The return home, for John and Margaret, the bright students of the 1910 class, was dismal and heavy with a sense of defeat. Broken in health, a career foundering, John had nothing to show for their years in Vancouver except the charming toddler. Margaret choked back her early pregnancy nausea, trying to keep people from knowing that she was so inopportunely with child. They moved in with Grammie and Grampa Abbott temporarily. There was no money, and John had not yet established his name with American papers. His dilemma reached Frost, who hastened to write from Littleton, New Hampshire, on May 20, 1915:

"Just you hold on a bit till I know where I stand with my Boston friends and I will do so for you (and more also) as I needed someone to do for me, when I was your age. At least I will try. There are a dozen sorts of things you could do and make more money in a week than I ever could in a year. Don't count on me too much, but, as I say, I will try."

Rob managed a trip south from Franconia, where he was settling the business of buying a farm. It was a renewal of the kind of talk they'd enjoyed in previous years, but with the added breadth of experience that living on foreign soil provides. There were the special conditions of the world. John had watched the depression in Vancouver, the bread lines, the unemployed; and then felt the fervor with which the men of Vancouver entered the war. Vancouver's boys were the fodder at Ypres in April of 1915, when the Germans launched their first gas attack. Their heroic action of holding the line for seventy hours and breaking two German divisions won the Vancouver battalion the Victoria Cross, but the cost in casualties was three men out of five. Frost, so recently in England, and John, in Canada, could not read reports with American feelings of "neutrality." When the *Lusitania* was sunk by a German submarine on May 7, 1915,

Rob wrote his immediate reaction in a letter he sent the next morning from Malden, Massachusetts:

"I got through my Phi Beta Kappa and my speech before the Authors Club but what does it matter about me? I'm sick this morning with hate of England and America because they have let this happen and will do nothing to punish the Germans. They can do nothing. I have no faith in any of them. Germany will somehow come out of this war if not completely victorious at least formidable and needing only time to get wind for another round. Dammit.

I can't get away till some day next week.

Rob

What a world it is."

Frost, returning to the farm where he was putting down roots, summed up his view when he wrote John about June 2nd:

"We expect to be in this place [Franconia] from now on for a while. It will have to do. I think the war may end in five years in favor of the Germans. In that case Canada will join us to save herself, and all the British will steal away over here to live. North America will become the larger island of the English-speakers of the world. Maybe you don't see it as I do. But the prophecy stands. I wish I had been able to do it in ink, so that it would be more permanently of record, but I am off here by the Gale river with nothing but water to dip into if I had a pen, and all I have is a pencil.

It was good to see you all. Take care of yourself or I

shall transfer to the baby all the ambitions I have had for you."

In the same letter was enclosed a note from Elinor. The women shared their closer concerns, children and home, though Margaret had to be satisfied with "living with the folks" in Derry. Even before Elinor set the Franconia farm in order, she wrote Margaret:

"I have been thinking every day since Rob got home that the farm business would be settled, and that I would write to you as soon as it was settled, to see if you couldn't come immediately for a visit. But the owner of the farm has given us a lot of trouble. He has told all sorts of lies and it has taken time to bring him to terms. Every two or three days we have thought that it was all up, and that we would have to begin to hunt elsewhere, and it has kept us very nervous. Now, however, we are really on the point of moving. The man comes for the trunks tomorrow. The farm is only 3 miles from here, you know. The furniture hasn't come up from Plymouth yet, but it will probably come the last of the week, and the people who are moving out can leave enough beds for us to manage with until then. We are all eager to get there, and it has been very hard waiting.

Now can't you and John and the baby come for a long visit, a month at least. You can't imagine how much I want to see you all. We shall all be terribly disappointed if you cannot, but Rob says he is afraid John has made arrangements with his father to go to the Raymond farm. Couldn't you put it off for a time? I think the mountain air would do John a great deal of good and we all want to see you and John and the baby so very much. Rob says you have a lovely baby. Rob and I are anxious, also, to know John's plans for the future, and to consider if there isn't some possible way for us to help. If only we had more money. Of course it is a great pleasure to know there are so many people reading and liking Robert's books, but sometimes one can't help feeling there ought to be some money in it as well as reputation. Perhaps there will be in time.

Why hasn't John written since Rob came home? I hope you are neither of you ill. Please answer this letter by the next mail and say you will come some day next week.

I think we shall enjoy our new home very much. I wish the house was just a little larger, but it's such a cheerful, cosy place that I am willing to endure some inconveniences. The view is very fine, and the village of Franconia is exceptionally attractive. All I ask is that the children will like the school there and will find a few nice children for companions. They have been out of school for so long that it will be a bit difficult for them to fit in, I fear, and I tremble at the possibility of their disliking the whole place, and if they *should*—well, it would be still harder to sell the farm than it has been to buy it, I am afraid.

I am too tired to write any more tonight. I have been working very hard washing blankets all day. Do forgive me for not answering your letter before, but I have been too restless to write letters, and more than that, I have been very busy sewing. The children were quite destitute of clothes; they grow so fast that I cannot keep them respectable. How glad I am that you are not out west.

But if you cannot come to see us, we are not much better off than if you were there. Are you going to have another baby, Margaret? Rob said he thought not. Are you much stronger than when you came home? I want to know all about your life out there and to talk over so many things with you. Say you will come, won't you?

We all send much love,

Affectionately yours,

Elinor

Send your letter to Franconia, Box 82. If you can come, we'll pay your fare one way, for I know it's a long distance to come. Rob thinks he has almost enough mileage to get you here, and we'll send it along if you say the word.

E.F."

The invitation was not answered. Margaret's strength was limited, drained by her energetic youngster, and the expected new baby was growing heavier. But most of all, she hated the feeling of failure, of having to be "taken in" by her family. The move to the Bartlett summer farm in the Pawtuckaway mountains helped their need for independence, but the privacy Margaret hoped for was not found there. John's younger brother, Bob, home for the summer from Dartmouth, spent a good part of the summer on the farm with a college friend guest "making fudge," as Margaret used to tell the story, "and not fixing the roof when the sun was out, because it didn't need it, and then not being able to fix it when it rained because it was wet."

John did a little writing. A few pennies came in from articles, but, mostly, John was seeking relief from asthma, trying to loosen its grip and keep his energy from being consumed. The haying that had been the purpose of the farm had yielded less and less each year, and John had put in a crop of beans, hoping to improve the soil, but he played with the thought of what beans by the bushel might bring on the market.

Few visitors made the eight-mile trip to see them, and Margaret was grateful for any caller. She would find some delicacy to present: wild strawberries, a bit of homemade jam, or the wild honey she gave to Elinor who found her way there in order to visit. Margaret's anxieties for herself, not knowing where they would live when summer was over or where the new baby would be born or when John would be strong enough to work, must have spilled over to Elinor, and back to Rob. Elinor knew the enveloping loneliness of bearing children on an isolated farm. Rob's concern for "the young folks" was immediate. He wrote from Franconia on August 8, 1915:

"I feel as if we had gone and done it in getting settled so near and yet so far. How much better off are we than when we were 6000 miles apart? I speak on some such assumption as that we both need each other of course. I know I need you or someone like you dating back to the days when my friends were those who had brains enough to judge me for themselves. I have lately been piled on top of by a lot of people who mistake their appreciation of my reviews for an understanding of me. As an honest man I am not a little disturbed by it all. I long for something old and sure to cling to.

Is this the way it stands, that I will have to go to you

if I want your company? You positively wont think of trying it up here for your asthma? I see a possibility of my getting south to farm sooner or later. I am not going to be satisfied with just grass-farming. But this place will have to serve for a year or two or until I am rich enough to let it lie idle all but two or three months in the year. I should always want to keep it as a summer resort. I wish it were so we could have it together. We could be neighbors in some good fruit region down your way and up here we could all live together for the hay fever season. Wouldn't that be about right?

My scheme for a summer literary camp here is on its way toward realization. I'll tell you more of it soon if it interests you.

Elinor had the pleasantest time with you on your mountain. I have been sick to see you ever since she came home with the little box of wild honey. Why would you live in such a lonely place without benefit of teachers where I couldn't have joined you even if I had tried to make my plans harmonize with yours? It's rotten—too rotten to go on about. Say something helpful in your next letter."

Late in August Rob managed a trip south to Raymond. John's outlook was bleak and desperate. The summer was running out, and with it, the free rent. Moving in with either set of parents was an intolerable thought, an admission of defeat; they wanted their own home, and the new baby, the doctor's fee, all such expenses were coming up, with only a trickle of money from the writing. Even if his health were better, John deplored the thought of returning to newspaper work. He'd had his fill, but traveling along a winter countryside in search of farm and poultry articles hardly seemed practical. Maybe he should give up writing, turn farmer. Ideas would come, then the wheezing, the sleepless nights, exhaustion. Events would not wait for him to catch his breath. In such a state of "touching bottom," Rob walked with John over the country roads. They talked as they had in the days before John had gone West.

Returning to Franconia, Rob impulsively sent a brief note, on August 24th, back to "John-a" suffering in the darkness of the whale's belly.

"You're a good one—and a deep. I don't pretend to have fathomed you on this visit; but I got down into you far enough for my purpose: I know what I know. All I say is: you'll do. We had good talks. I like you and everything about and around you."

As fall came on, John's tension under these circumstances reached a literally explosive level. Grammie Abbott had come, bringing fresh eggs and worry, of course, over "what is poor Margaret going to do unless you come to live with us." The worry was real, but John was not in the mood to hear about it. And then little Forrest had pulled over the carton of eggs, breaking each and every one—such a flurry in the kitchen. Grammie and the eggs; Margaret comforting Forrest. John had been fussing with the old shotgun he had (on one occasion, anyway) used to scare deer away from the bean patch. The gun went off, with no damage other than severe fright and disapproval from the women. A letter from Rob, dated September 9, 1915, was John's only relief:

"No it is not among the fat-headed things I have done to have fired off a revolver that wasn't loaded and almost killed my fat mother-in-law.

You wont believe it, but I tell you all the same that I was certain sure you were getting too gay with that weapon. You see I do draw the line somewhere in folly. I never intend to do anything too fatally conclusive. I wouldn't for instance encourage any one to shoot me with an empty gun just to show how careless I was of appearances. I would take some other and less final way of asserting my recklessness. After all I am but a timid calculating soul always intent on the main chance. I always mean to win. All that distinguishes me from the others that mean to win or from some others is my patience. I am perfectly willing to wait fifty seventy five or a thousand years as the fates may decree. I might be willing to be cut off at almost any time (I *might*) but it would have to be for something. I do nothing for nothing.

Frost has twice hit our garden hard and there is nothing more to look for from it but beets turnips and cauli-flowers. So it goes. I doubt if what we have had from our summer's planting has cost us any more than it would have in the market.

I wish it lay with me to straighten out the question of where you are going to live this winter. I wish it lay with me to straighten out you.

You should have seen me doing that eight miles to Raymond, mosquito-driven, scoffed at by people in wagons, but coming through with half an hour to spare.

I hope there was another journey or two left in the bicycle. Anyway I must have improved the walls by drying them up considerably.

Enjoy yourself but try to be good. Affectionately

R.

A large fat man that morning in a sagging light buggy stopped and stopped me dead still before he put the deliberate question: I wish you'd tell me what the difference is between riding a bicycle and walking."

By mid-September John had managed to scrape together enough pennies to rent a farmhouse at the top of Long Hill, about a mile from the center of Raymond. A wagon was to be sent to take Margaret to her new home. She waited, fearful the baby would be born "any minute," until the wagon finally arrived in first week of October. "It's a wonder the baby wasn't born beside the road!" she'd say, remembering the ride over the rutted road, lurching on the hard, springless board seat, and wondering why no one had been thoughtful enough to suggest they send a buggy for her.

John T. Bartlett III was born the fifteenth of October, with John riding in the night on his bicycle to summon the doctor. The memories of John's birth were not happy ones. He was a big baby for Margaret's small frame, and the doctor "had whisky on his breath. He would have spread old newspapers on the bed if I hadn't already sterilized some sheets in the oven!" The newborn Johnny was put in a bassinet improvised from a pulled-out bureau drawer. Margaret was more exhausted by this birth than any of the others, but she came through, and the second son was lusty and strong. John flashed the news to Rob.

About October 21, 1915, John received a reply from Rob in Franconia:

"Be good to him! And that doesn't mean simply not to write poetry for a living. For his sake you are bound to shun *every* folly, ginseng, Belgian hares, squabs, wonder-berries, mushrooms, Orpingtons, alfalfa, Angora goats, Mexican rubber stock for the small investor and the Honduras Lottery. Those are the things as well as poetry you have to have in mind when you pray saying 'Lead us not into temptation but deliver us from evil.' For now you are a father, twice over and must give up childish ways in favor of your children. I'd like to be your wife for about five minutes some day till I could knock the whole duty of the responsible head of a family into your head. I'd have no more of this romancing in agriculture. I speak partly from concern for your own future. Suppose your sons grow up to be sensible men. How will you feel when you begin to realize that they were judging you. They will be earning fifty seventy-five a hundred dollars a week. About that time you will have got round to skunks and will be starting a skunk farm—chuck full of your subject, all the lore of deodorizing skunk skins so as not to make the hair come out and of picking up a skunk by the tail without consequences—full of figures too such as these: Assuming that a skunk will produce twenty five pole kittens in an off year it ought to do say one fourth as well as a rabbit and we all know what a rabbit will do—but assuming to be on the safe side that it will produce no more than twenty-five and that except for a considerable loss in overalls which you have had to bury without benefit of clergy, the twenty-five have cost you nothing to rear and the market price of a pelt—why it ought to be two dollars if its a (s)cent oughtn't it and so on. How will you feel, say, if when you talk like that you catch your two solid and citizenly sons winking at each other on the sly? You will feel like as if it was a tragedy if I may speak like another Reynolds. You will feel as if you had vainly wasted your life in vain. The moral is that the least little thing starts me moralizing these days and this is not a little thing. Bless the whole lot of you. The score now stands 4 to 2 in favor of us. But the game is young yet, or at least you are."

Winter came on, a winter of worry; John and Margaret living closely on a marginal subsistence, and Frost with grave concern for Elinor's health. "The game is young yet," he'd hinted in his letter, a reference to a late pregnancy of Elinor's which ended in a miscarriage. In December he wrote:

"Dear Johnah:
We are suddenly out of our misery and nothing to show for it. It has been so much worse than we remembered it from times past that we had begun to suspect that something must be wrong. It turns out that nothing has been right for three months. Elinor has been unspeakably sick. But I think we are safely out of the woods now. I will write in a better frame of mind when I write again."

In spite of his asthma John did venture out to gather material for articles. It was a frugal living, making do with Pa Abbott's used razor blades, stewing dried prunes and apricots, but "I could always buy my own thread," Margaret said with pride, "for mending frayed collars and turning cuffs, and making over John's old shirts for Forrest." But she hated being alone with the babies on long winter nights. Not many traveled the steep hill in the cold and snow to visit, except for John's niece, Priscilla, who didn't mind the winter trek after school, although it worried her mother and grandmother for her to climb "that awful hill." Sometimes she'd stay over-night, if John were away and Margaret were alone, and they'd stay up late, sitting in the snug warmth of the kitchen and playing games to put off climbing between the cold sheets of the bed in the icy bedroom.

Sometimes John would place an article that he had doubts about; at other times a good one would go amiss. He still sold more to British Columbia publications, writing from notes he'd made before he left the West, than to New England papers. But they made it through the winter, with thoughts of finding a mountain climate in the summer, both to relieve the asthma and to find new sources of farming material. He wrote Rob to sound out the possibilities near Franconia. Rob answered in May of 1916:

"A letter once in a while can do no harm to him that sends or him that receives, though damn letters as a rule. There are a few people I might enjoy writing to if there weren't so many I had to write to. I remember the time when I looked forward to an evening of writing to you. I'd rather see you now than write to you. Strange, aint it?

Of course there's a whole lot about the art of writing that none of us ever masters. We all remain duffers and properly dissatisfied with ourselves. I'm not speaking of the art of letter writing but of the longer art of writing for the Country Gentleman. It is touch and go with any of us. Now we get it for a little run of sentences and now we don't.

There are tones of voice that mean more than words. Sentences may be so shaped as definitely to indicate these tones. Only when we are making sentences so shaped are we really writing. And that is flat. A sentence *must* convey a meaning by tone of voice and it must be the particular meaning the writer intended. The reader must have no choice in the matter. The tone of voice and its meaning must be in black and white on the page.

I will take a look around for you up here. I had counted on the Lynches. But from what I hear they may be too crowded to take any one in this summer. A son has come home with his family to stay with them for a while. I'll see them however as soon as I get back from this trip. I'll find somebody to take you in.

I wish I could see you this time. But I can't honestly. I'm longer away than I ought to be every time as it is. I'll leave here on the 2 P.M. tomorrow—leave the house at 1 P.M.—get to Boston at 9 P.M., take the midnight for New York, reach New York at 7 A.M. Thursday, take the 8 A.M. for Philadelphia, reach Philadelphia at 10 A.M., read, get away on the midnight for New York, take 7 A.M. train Friday for Providence, read, sleep, take early morning train for Boston for a little business and then scoot home. You see the kind of jaunts I take. The Harvard one on the 19th will be the last. (You must get down to Boston for that to please me.) Some time in July the family will move down to Plymouth for a week while I talk to the summer school seven or eight times. But that is another thing. None of us will suffer by that particularly.

Well old man *stay* on the map. Elinor will write and tell Margaret what to do. But you stay on the map."

John and Rob didn't get together for a talk until summer, when John left Margaret and the boys and went to Bethlehem, not far from Franconia, with his mother, sister Ada, and Priscilla. These were Margaret's unhappiest years, with a growing resentment of Grandmother Bartlett's concern for "poor John, you mustn't overdo." She felt "Gargie," as Forrest called his grandmother, "whisked him off" to the mountains with little thought for her, although she was never one to "find fault." Occasional classmates calling on Margaret always found her cheerful and pleasant, if tired-looking; and she would bake cookies or make chocolate fudge if she knew someone were coming.

But there were fears, being alone on the farm. Forrest, one bright, early summer day, had come running in from the field where the grass was nearly as tall as he, crying that something had bitten him. All she could find were two pin-point pricks behind his ear, made by a snake or an insect, she didn't know. But the tears were not long-lasting; it seemed just another brief hurt in a small child's day. During the night, Margaret awoke for no apparent reason, and checking Forrest found that he was cold and pale and unresponsive. She acted as instinct dictated, moving him, shaking him awake, almost seeming to shake life back into him and bring color into his white cheeks. The crisis passed and he was running about the next day quite as usual. But the fright, the questions: "what woke me?" and "what if I hadn't looked at Forrest!" lingered and shriveled her as night drew on, while she dreaded John's absences.

John was scouting out a new place to live; but it was convenient now to stay in Bethlehem with his mother, who'd rented a place for the summer to find relief from her own hay fever. Ada and her daughter, Priscilla, were with her, and, of course, there was room for John. Rob came over one night to see a baseball game between Franconia and Bethlehem, and stayed for supper, sitting in the kitchen to talk. Priscilla, leafing through a book of illustrated Shakespeare, made a game of dressing up in bedspreads, table covers, and whatever she could find, and parading in front of the grown-ups, asking them to guess which Shakesperian heroine she was portraying. Rob stayed till midnight, then walked the eight miles back to Franconia.

Toward the end of the summer John received a letter from Margaret saying the boys were both sick. There had been cases of infantile paralysis that summer, and John, immediately fearing the worst, started back to Raymond on the run. Priscilla went to the station with him, and when he discovered he did not have money for the fare, she offered him her summer's savings, about $2.50, which he gratefully accepted in order to get home. Money from any source was needed to get by.

The young couple had to move to a higher climate, and Margaret felt improvement in the asthma would come not only from the higher altitude but getting away from the generous and goodhearted but protective mother who catered to John's illness. The move, when it was made, was a quick, impulsive jump to Warner, New Hampshire. John had apparently let Frost know he was trying to borrow some money from his family to make the move. Not expecting to leave so suddenly, plans to meet Frost in Raymond somehow went amiss. On September 28, 1916, Frost wrote from Franconia:

"Twice. The first time before you cleared out for good, I judge. I don't know where you all were. It was late in the afternoon and showery. Not finding anyone around I didn't dare to wait for you when it meant missing a chance to ride home.

I supposed something abysmal was up. I didn't blame you, and you don't care if I did: which is where you are right. You seem to feel as if you had everything to gain and nothing to lose by anything that can happen.

I'm feeling advisory. You sign all the notes they will let you so long as you are paid to. I shouldn't suppose it was recovering on them they were thinking of. They simply want it to be as if you were getting now what would be coming to you if your parents ever died. Lets hope they'll never die. You don't care when they die if you can only begin to inherit their property now when you want it.

Beastly way to talk. Sounds as if I was on your side instead of your parents'. I'm not. I hold with them it's time you did something to get well. I share their anxiety for you. Get well. Nothing else matters. You are playing nearer the edge than ever I dared play.

I wish you could have come here to live. But I can see the Advantage of Claremont, pop 8000, alt 500, and not too far from what's going on. I shouldn't root too deeply there for fear the climate would wear out and you might want to come to the mountains.

I've bet good money on you: so take care of yourself on my account—not to please me but to save me loss. Have you done anything to stop the mouth breathing?"

The house in Warner was Margaret's one really happy memory of the two years in New Hampshire. "It was a lovely white cottage, with a picket fence and red roses." They had their privacy again, cherished by Margaret. The blunt, well-meaning remarks of her mother-in-law she felt as sharp criticism. "You're too thin, Margaret. Ought to put a little meat on your bones!" she'd say, and Margaret would shrink inside. They bought a few hens, both as a gesture to economy, but also for the New England sense of being settled. John still made interviewing trips, went back to Raymond, and on such jaunts tried to catch Frost, also on the wing with lectures to give. Again their efforts to meet failed to work out. Frost, in a letter dated simply Winter, 1916, wrote:

"I was badly disappointed when you failed me at the eleven o'clock train. I stood on the step as we pulled out hoping you were going to turn up from somewhere on the run and catch the train at the last minute. I was on the point of dropping off when you didn't, but I remembered my luggage which I had left in my seat where I couldn't get it and get off before we were moving too fast. I assumed of course that you had been delayed by some accident and might think of coming along on the next train. At Haverhill I stopped over and telephoned back to the station agent at Exeter to ask him to look and see if he saw the likes of you about the station. I boarded the next train when it came but there was no you on it. So I gave you up. I got the leaves you tore out of your note-book three or four days afterward at home in Franconia.

The Exeter evening was better than the Dartmouth dinner. I never can tell where I am going to like my job. Lawrence was rather a success: most of the schools and colleges have been. The Dartmouth Dinner was for the politicians. I felt rather lost with my brief poem in all the smoke and noise. I would do better another time; for I would bargain for an early place on the program and should know from experience how to make more of my voice and manner. I wasnt particularly good at the New York Dinner either. There I struck too serious a note. Dinners are all new to me.

There was a reasonable chance of our dropping in on you at Raymond as we came along up. But that went glimmering when Elinor was taken sick in Cambridge and I had to leave her there in bed while I came home to see about the children. I had no sooner got here than I was taken sick myself and the children had to see about me. So our bust busted. Better luck next time!

Fifteen below here this morning. Twenty-five below the morning I left for my last tour. Hope it will moderate before my next which begins in five days. I jump clear to Schenectady this time.

Be good to your Rhode Island Reds!"

By the winter of 1917 John had managed a tenuous hold, though his asthma remained unrelenting. In January it became evident that Margaret's fatigue and loss of weight was more than just the tiredness of caring for two small boys. She had a cough, and the telltale flecks of red—trouble in her lungs. The doctors confirmed their fear: tuberculosis. Grandmother Bartlett immediately went to Warner to help nurse Margaret, even though she had an arm in splints, and when she left, Priscilla went for a weekend to help out. Margaret wouldn't stay in bed. She felt no worse for having a diagnosis made; she had been worn out for two years. The news traveled to Frost, now at Amherst where he'd gone back to teaching. He wrote from there on February 13, 1917:

"You will have heard I am teaching again. I have to do something for the country once in so often even when it isn't at war.

And speaking of war, what kind of a trouble have you children got yourselves into? Didn't I tell you you would have to stick at nothing to get over these hard times? You have still your reserves—things you won't give up. But you'll have to give up everything for a little while. Those boys ought to go on a visit to one of their grandmothers. You can do a lot for them. But if you're the least like me, not enough to take them entirely off Margaret's mind. She's got to be relieved of them to get well. That's sure. She can't afford to be foolish for a moment, and neither can you. I have seen right in my own family one person lost by not taking instant and out-and-out measures and another person saved by taking them. The business can go either way you want it to, but I'm afraid generally as most of us are entangled in life and obligations, it inclines to go the wrong way. Cut and run away from every care: that is the rule.

Nothing else will do. No faltering. I saw the way my father fed his hopes on one concession after another. It was my first tragedy.

Some time when you are near a bank will you cash this check and use it for any little thing for Margaret? You can pay it back to me when I am old and neglected, with interest at one tenth of one per cent—or as much more as you like if I am very much neglected."

Margaret accepted her illness quite passively. As she'd tell the story, "I was ready to die there, in the white bungalow with the roses on the fence. I had it all planned, that Gargie would take Forrest, and red-cheeked, chunky Johnny would go to Grammie Abbott." But John was in no frame of mind to accept that kind of fate. There was no money for hospital care. The only hope for both of them was a complete change of climate; no half-measure New Hampshire mountain but the high and dry air of Arizona or Colorado. He wrote his father asking for money to stake him, so to speak, on a move West.

John kept the answer from his father, dated April 16, 1917, among the Frost letters.

"When any of my children ask me for help or for money I am always inclined to reply affirmatively. I have always done so. Things are different now. I have grown old and I find that the preparations which I have desired to make against the time when I can no longer work are far from complete and I am in great need of present money. . . . I must now have for my own use all that I can earn. It is very little and must constantly diminish as I grow less and less able to manage my work . . .

"It is time for you to learn to depend upon yourself

for all the things you are to have. To this day you have not learned to rely upon yourself and to keep your expenditures within such income as you can produce. You have looked to me or to your mother or to both of us. I cannot yet believe you have not sufficient ability to accomplish this result. You have been impeded by ill health, it is true, but the greater impediment has lain in the fact that you have never felt obliged to live within what you could earn. You can do it, however, and if you are ever to get anywhere, you must do it. I have faith in you and believe you can make good, and, when you have done it, the same feelings will fill your heart that you had when you licked certain boys years ago. . . ."

John never asked anybody for money again. He worked as best he could, scraping together enough to keep up with bills, but could not get ahead in his plan for moving West. In April the United States entered the war, and John immediately sought out opportunities to write for the Committee on Public Information. Maybe he could find government work. Plans, still nebulous, were shaping up, though he found no support. His father's health was not good, and he'd already given his answer on the money question. His mother, fearing for John's health, discouraged a far-away move for her favorite son or even talk of steady government work. Only Rob could see wisdom in the move. He wrote on April 25, 1917, from Amherst:

"It seems to me the best thing might be for you to go west and see what you could find to do out there. Part-time work if you could find it would be the idea. You must save as much as you can of yourself for the writing;

because the writing is going to be the whole thing with you sooner or later—I have no doubt sooner. For the present though and to shake off these family troubles which may have a good deal to do with keeping you down in health, I should see what I could do with a limited regular job under favorable climactic conditions. I should want it to be for short hours so that you could give one hour a day to writing. And I should make the one hour a hard and fast rule. You can do a lot in an hour if you come to it with your thoughts already somewhat shaped—and you can even if your thoughts aren't shaped. I should hold myself in awhile for health's sake. You've got to tighten up on your follies no matter how amicable or admirable they may be.

This is the advice you ask for. I should know better what to tell you to do with yourself if I were surer what I ought to do with myself in the present crisis.

To put it in few words, my program for you would be five hours work a day for small pay and one hour's writing in some part of the country where you will breathe easier.

Your mother's letter does not please me, though no doubt she means well. She appears willing that you should die for your father and mother and sisters and brother, but glad that your asthma keeps you from dying for your country. Your situation becomes ignominious. You must win your independence, I feel sure, before you can hope to get well for good.

This is a funny world."

More than just words, Rob sent fifty dollars, enough to pay the fare west to Colorado. They saved the money,

John Bartlett was an honor student, a three-letter man in athletics, and class president his senior year, 1910, at Pinkerton Academy.

Frost's class graduated from Pinkerton in 1910, with
Margaret Abbott the undisputed valedictorian.

Robert Frost in Franconia about 1915. This was around the same time that John went to Bethlehem to stay with Mother Bartlett and his sister.

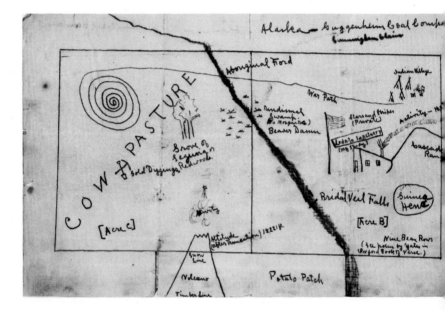

University of Virginia Library

Even before John and Margaret were married, Frost had talked about trying Vancouver. In one of his letters, around 1912, he sketched this "Three-Acre Desideratum" map, showing the successful John on Acre A (above) and his own lean-to sanctuary on Acre B.

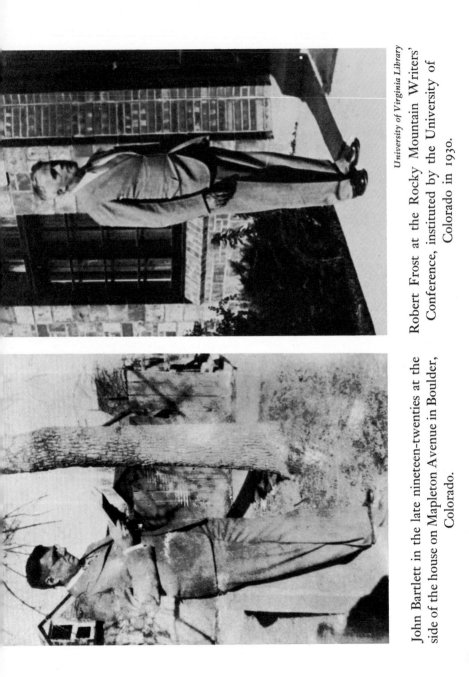

Robert Frost at the Rocky Mountain Writers' Conference, instituted by the University of Colorado in 1930.

John Bartlett in the late nineteen-twenties at the side of the house on Mapleton Avenue in Boulder, Colorado.

The whole Bartlett family — Richard and Margaret Emily (in the front row); Forrest, Margaret and John, and John, Jr. (in the back row).

Charles F. Snow

By 1938 John was thoroughly involved in politics and Margaret was running the family's business affairs.

Charles F. Snow

not ready to leave until they managed to clear every debt. In August of 1917 they wrote Rob, back in Franconia for the summer, of their final plans. He replied on August 13th:

"I dont see how I am to get down to see you—I really don't. Elinor has been sick for a long time. We dont know what is the matter with her unless it is something that may come to an end abruptly at any moment. I ought not to be far from her—at any rate till we know more certainly how it is with her. We are all going back to Amherst next month. But you have determined to get away before then. I very much want a talk with you. Would you come here for a day and night if I would foot the bill? This in haste on impulse."

There was not a moment to spare for a good-bye trip to Franconia. They boarded the train heading West, this time with two eager, towheaded youngsters dancing wide-eyed to the excitement of a big transcontinental passenger train with its engine hissing steam. Margaret, thin, but with her hair carefully braided and wound around her head like a crown, was too tired to worry any further than "changing trains in Chicago." John carried the bag with his patent medicine asthma powder "for emergency relief." No one waited at the other end of their journey, but with finality and no backward looks they left their home in New Hampshire for good.

V

Colorado,
1917-1930

Margaret never forgot the "change in Chicago," as if changing trains were as perilous as leaping from one side of a chasm to the other, the awful moment of suspension at having left the ties of New Hampshire and before settling down on the other side. Then there was the long ride west, the countryside of the mid-West farming belt petering out to the vast stretches of plains, empty flatness in every direction, with the telephone poles like an endless single file of soldiers marching into the distance until they dropped off the edge of the world; a train from somewhere to nowhere. In later automobile trips, coming back to the Rockies from across the prairie, Margaret looked for the "first glimpse" of the purple haze that would gradually take shape and grow to the size of a magnificent backdrop, recalling her first excitement, her awakening of hope on the first trip to Colorado in 1917. The snow-capped peaks jutting sky high with massive strength, dignity, and quietness were like the capital letter at the beginning of a sentence. Instead of an end, they found at the foot of the Rocky Mountains a permanent home and the beginning of a successful life.

They settled first in Fort Collins, renting a small frame house; and instead of seeking medical help they simply opened wide the windows and breathed the free, clear Colorado air. Margaret wrote of that first year, "John was unable to do interviewing—could, in fact, work at writing only an hour or two a day. What he wrote he had to dig out of notebooks he had used while interviewing for agricultural papers the two years we were back in New England; little kinks for farm papers, the popular mechanics papers, the boy's papers. But these items brought in little money. We hit bottom in January 1918, when our little black record book showed *New England Homestead*, $1.45; *Nebraska Farmer*, $2.60; *Rural Life*, $1.00; *Nebraska Farmer*, $3.30; *Farm Life*, $3.00; *Fruitgrower*, $2.00; *Successful Farming*, $8.65; and *Farm and Fireside*, $3.00. Total: $25.00.

"Nobody in the East knew how close we came to a steady pinto bean diet. We learned to tuck a meadowlark's song into an envelope home, a snatch of Colorado blue sky, a whiff of clear, cool Colorado air, pleasing bits about the two little boys. . . ."

But the tiny nuggets mined from the notebooks added up, even at the rate of half a cent a word, which was the going price with most publications. Margaret began writing, too, articles on child-rearing and household hints for home departments, little "moralities" for Sunday-school papers. Skimpy years, but a worn bank book kept in the desk drawer showed small but fairly regular deposits of five, seven, and ten dollars in the Fort Collins bank.

Margaret never talked about her own illness, which had been a prime factor in their moving. The TB apparently "cured itself," and her belief in the healing powers of Colorado air never wavered. She couldn't breathe unless windows were opened wide every night, even in sub-zero weather, and every morning doors and windows were opened to "clear the air." Because both of them were thin, a rich pot of cocoa was their breakfast drink, never coffee. No matter how few the pennies for food, they had "real butter" on the table; and their strength increased. With her first earnings Margaret bought a Sears, Roebuck "Minnesota-A" sewing machine, mending worn clothes with care and "making over" shirts and trousers for the boys, a labor of love, but regarded suspiciously by Johnny who'd ask, "this shirt second-hand?" and refused to wear the hand-me-downs. She never could understand Johnny.

In the spring of 1919 they bought some chickens from a family down the street, delivered in a gunny sack by one of the boys whose big brother had just had scarlet fever. Fresh eggs and Sunday dinners may have helped their economy. The scarlet fever which struck the whole family did not. The doctor who took care of them, noticing the frugal furnishings, the ancient stove with the broken hinge, and learning that John was a writer with no employer, assumed the young couple was "needy." A practical nurse hired by the county was sent to help out, a service they were too sick to deny, but when the doctor had a second-hand stove delivered to the door John and Margaret were well enough to stand on their own feet and "turn back charity!" Such was their pride in making their own way that when no bill was sent for the nurse, John went to the city hall and demanded to pay for her services, even though it took a large portion of their hundred-dollar savings.

Still incensed by being considered charity, John aired his feelings in a post card to Rob, who apparently misunderstood the message and had to be set straight. On April 7, 1919, Rob wrote from Franconia:

"You have yourself partly to blame for writing me such a merry little post card. But I suppose it was the best you could do you poor boy if you were sick in bed. Gee I didn't get what you were trying to tell me did I? Let's see what I did think you were saying: that Margaret had got an editorial job sifting poetry of a Farm Journal and that you had all been sick but had come through all right and things were going well. To me the post card balanced up to the good. So far from intending to make light of your bad luck I was really making gay over your good luck. My mistake began and ended with my misreading of the post card. Don't be so cramped and cryptic another time. You have to be pretty broad and outright with an old fellow like me. . . .

Isn't it rotten that you should have had such a time? What right had all those associated charities in on top of you? Or did you have to have them in? Upwards of one hundred dollars a month sounds not so bad when you have your own garden and hens. Tell me more about it.

You can't be so wretched. Did the doctor call in the charities? Are the neighbors gossiping about you because you are sick and literary? Hall makes *me* sick. Say right up and down, do you want some money now. Say how much and let me see how much of it I can rake together.

Do you mean by 'cards on the table' any kind of personal news good or bad? Well we haven't had Scarlet Fever but we have had five cases of influenza out of a possible six all of them bad enough but only one and that mine anywhere near fatal. Irma was sick in October and is not fully recovered yet. The year for us at Amherst was unsatisfactory what with all this sickness and the unsettlement in the college due to the war. We came away with a bad enough conscience about the money we had taken for no work to speak of and yet after all not so bad either; we managed to blame others as much as ourselves for the way things had gone. We would almost as soon have gone without the money if we could have been out of the confusion of a war-wrecked college—a rather unpatriotic one at that. Maybe we could have been writing something if we hadn't been killing time down there on salary.

I have gone rather easy on the writing for the two years last past. Breath-weight [William Stanley Braithwaite] had no choice in the matter of taking or leaving any poetry of mine for his anthology. There was none. Nary a drop. I have shown not a poem to an editor since I gave The Axe Helve to The Atlantic summer before last. So that lets the [secret] out. (The first part of the Axe-Helve was a good poem the last part not. You probably didn't see it.)

Not that I've absolutely stopped writing. I do a little and let it lie around where I can enjoy it for its own sake and not for what some [fool] may think of it. By and bye we will show ourselves again. No hurry. Wait till [they've] have had time to try themselves on An Old Man's Winter Night and The Gum Gatherer. It's up to them to read as much as it is to me to write.

We are into White Wyandottes again fifteen deep. We haven't had enough experience any of us with Barred Plymouth Rock to qualify as experts in White Leghorns though we did do awfully well with about a dozen B.P.R.'s all one winter. Which puts an idea into my head. How would a book be on the Barred Plymouth Rock by the Plymouth Rock Bard? Thus is literature made. Watch me.

Wet cold and wild on this mountain still. I hate to have you so far off out there and sometimes wish I could say Come on East and try this Franconia or Sugar Hill climate for the various ills your flesh is heir to. But I don't know. You know best anyway. Are you on the whole better in the throat and lungs, both of you? Shall you ever venture East again? I wish I could see you. I get as far as Chicago about once a year but though that seems a long way it isn't more than half way to you.

You mustn't write long letters. As you say letters are no good. You need your strength for other writing—just as I need mine. I have to nurse it out of myself always you know. Nerves nerves! It's the same with both of us only I won't claim it isn't worse with you. No you mustn't spend yourself in letters to me. What you must do though is tell me what you are writing and let me see some of it—yours and Margaret's both. This is per-emptory."

Still peeling from the scarlet fever, they were visited by a "thin, scrawny woman with loose hairs sticking like long black whiskers from under her rusty straw hat," who demanded her house back. She was the landlady who had lived in another town. Now she wanted to move back immediately and threatened to put them out, in the harsh manner of the witch in a fairy tale. The children were frightened, but John had already thought of moving to Denver, his interests having changed from agricultural news to business reports. His first house-hunting trip to Denver resulted only in the conviction that he could never be happy living in a big city.

Of course, there was precious little money for a move, their bank account having nearly gone to pay for the nurse. They were saved, this time, by a fifty-six dollar check from the *Nebraska Farmer*, the biggest they had ever received, payment for six articles "on acceptance" rather than the usual wait for "publication." With money for the move John went house-hunting again, stopping short of Denver in Boulder, a university town snuggled close to the foot of Flagstaff mountain. This was the place he wanted, and here he found a farm for rent nine miles east of town at Pleasant View. It was a dilapidated old house, originally painted red but weathered to a dusty dried-blood color, with a yard full of weeds and poplar trees, dying at the top. The view of the Rockies was magnificent, and the well water was "the best found any-where," although they had to walk to the outdoor pump to get it summer and winter.

Productivity increased at Pleasant View, with John entering the field of trade-journal writing. Monthly income, for all the rejection slips, never fell below a hundred dollars a month.

That summer, to their considerable pride, they were visited by John's parents, a final visit for his father who died the next year. They enjoyed walks over Colorado country roads and talk in the kitchen about friends, characters, and politicians. In the summer of 1919 Rob again wrote from Franconia, apparently having received magazine clippings from John:

". . . It will take the homesickness out of living away off so far from New Hampshire to have had your father and mother with you for a long stay. Your mother especially carries so much New Hampshire with her wherever she goes that I'm sure she is bound to leave a tone and atmosphere of it wherever she has come and gone. Both your father and mother are the best kind of folks. It's great they took the notion they could desert their clients and star boarders to go visiting their Western Son. (Chance there to do something with westering and sun but I've gone by it and it won't do to go back.)

Awful stuff some of the poor ladies write about us but I suppose it must be to earn a living. Possibly it's to see themselves in print. It can't advance them in fame or me either I should think. My publisher would say it might sell books. It sort of disseminates me. You could say that such a mouthful as you quote was me getting down to the women's clubs. That's only a guess. It's got so I don't see much that's said about me. It's understood with my publishers that I don't want to be bothered with either the pros or cons and I have never subscribed to a clipping agency. What reaches me leaks in by accident. Once in a while some editor sends some marked passage in his magazine about me. I take most of it rather badly—that is to say I am apt to wonder too long what it means and if there is anything to it whether friendly or unfriendly. There's better business I can be about. The main thing is to pursue the even tenor. I never wrote to write right: I wrote for the fun of it. That's all I can hope to write for. For the fun of it in the large sense—for the devil of it—to [place] myself where I could bother the critics, not where the critics could bother me. Of course they count in the long run. Sooner or later its theirs to dispose of me. I'm only concerned with the distant result. . . .

Being writers does give us certain freedoms and if it doesn't take us at least lets us go to interesting places to live. No place is out of the way to writers. And our kids get something out of this. It makes up to them for some losses. I can just see it making it up to the two boys as photographed."

John liked the life at Pleasant View. "Every other week I'd leave the farm, the chickens and the garden, and go to Denver or other interviewing territory. In three or four days I would be back, and as I worked up my articles from my notes, I felt myself the most independent person in the world. I didn't envy anybody."

Neighbors were a little suspicious, though, about the goings on, and once Margaret received a call from a government agent checking to see if they were engaged in spying activities, since they were obviously not farmers.

Dr. Farrington, the country doctor with the reddish Vandyke beard, who looked after Margaret's pregnancies (another boy, Richard, and myself, Margaret the second, were born in the Pleasant View years) and diagnosed measles and mumps, would often stay to visit a bit, picking up a magazine and turning to the page marked on the cover to find an article by one or the other of the Bartletts. "The old doctor's eyes would brighten as he saw one of our names, and with a smile he'd raise his hand, making a play at snatching an imaginary dollar. 'Wonderful!' he'd say, 'What an easy way to earn a living just picking dollars out of the air!' "

But it wasn't easy. They worked by quotas, so many words a week. For Margaret, it was a thousand words three nights a week. In later years, when she heard writers complain of ideas not coming, "My most effective cure," she told them, "was a bang on the head. In those farm days when I set myself to write three evenings a week, I'd approach the old green Oliver so weary after a long, long day of cleaning and cooking and caring for children (not even the convenience of a kitchen sink!) and conversation with an always-at-home husband, that when I turned the pure white sheet of paper into my machine, there'd not be a thought in my head. I'd try to think of something—an idea for an article, a germ of a children's story—but nothing would come. My head would nod; my eyes would close. Suddenly, bump! Down my forehead would crack on the high keybars. I'd shake my head; my nap was over, I was wide awake—there was a flash! I had my thought. I don't recall ever leaving the typewriter without completing my 750 to 1000 word story or article." They never sent samples to Rob or wrote many letters from the farm.

On October 16, 1920, Rob wrote from Arlington, Vermont:

"Word reaches us in a round-about way that you two and your offspring are beautiful. But that is not the same thing as the assurance directly from you. This is written to ask for your news—how you are and how you are working. I really must tell you again that I am anxious to see some of your literature. I wouldn't say so if I didn't mean it. Of course, if I were as anxious as a detective bureau to find out who blew up J. Pierpont Morgan and Co. I could subscribe to all the magazines going and read and read them till I found your signature or came on internal evidence that marked something as unmistakeably yours. You know you might say something that would give you away to me if to nobody else. As it is I confess I don't subscribe to a single magazine agricultural, religious political or neither. I'm too lazy to go hunting for you at large. I've waited patiently for some years for a glimpse of you in print and now in all friendliness and for the last time but ten I demand it. . . .

We couldn't think of going west or any further west than the western boundary of New England because I have to be where I can earn a little money by lecturing at colleges especially now that I have chucked Amherst. I served my time at Amherst (four years) the same as at Pinkerton; just to show that as the father of a family I could do what I had to and then turned to something I liked to do better. And now I or Carol and I or we'll say Carol is going to plant some apple trees at South Shaftsbury and dig in and grow up with them. Don't fear for us. The good God will take care of them that don't put on any airs.

There, now say something in reply."

Hours were precious though, with two new babies, and having once established their markets with the trade journals, they maintained a steady pace with their articles. They worked six days a week—Sunday was a day for rest. Evenings, John might walk with the boys up the road to the school or read books and magazines, if he'd written enough for the day. He always went to bed before Margaret, who seldom finished her tasks of the day before eleven o'clock. She was up again at seven in the morning to start the fire in the kitchen stove, and was well into the day when John appeared for breakfast at ten o'clock. Once, with an extra large check, John entertained farmerish thoughts of buying a cow to supply the family with milk, figuring the savings and added measure of health. Margaret was in no mind to add a cow to her cares. Chickens, a family of ducks (pets rather than produce), a cat, and two goats, Billy and Theda, were quite enough. She was weak with relief when John returned from his buying trip with a bicycle instead of a cow!

Frost had ventured west of the New England boundary in 1921, but only as far as Ann Arbor, Michigan, where he held the position of "Poet in Residence" at the University of Michigan. Correspondence was fitful.

In June of 1922 Rob wrote from Ann Arbor:

"I've been thinking about you lately and wondering what I could do to get a letter out of you. I suppose I could write a letter to you.

I'm still at Ann Arbor, Mich but the climax of annual improvements is about reached and it wont be many days before we book for home. We are Elinor and I. The children long since went ahead of us to set the hens and watch the apples and pears set themselves. Home is now South Shaftsbury Vermont about seventy miles south of Middlebury. So if I do get a letter out of you let it be addressed to me there.

Lets see you lived once for a little while in Vermont and once for a little while just across from it at Claremont. Where havent you and I lived for a little while? You've lived a pretty well settled life in Colorado— pretty well.

I guess I lived the longest I ever lived under the same roof on the farm at Derry I was seven years there. I think of you in many places. Remember the cold day when I put you over the hill on foot toward Littleton N.H.? I cant get over the strangeness of having been in so many places and yet remained one person. I have kept Raymond Derry and a hundred other New England towns alive in my memory not only by passing through them now and then but by thinking of buying a farm in one or another of them. I keep reading of them seriously in Strouts Farm Catalogue. I no sooner get settled in South Shaftsbury than I am at it again for some reason looking for another likely farm that could be bought right. I believe I'll end by buying a number of five hundred dollar farms in all sorts of places and holding them chiefly for the lumber on them but partly for a change of residence when I get restless. I could fix the houses up on them and rent them to medium poor city people who couldnt own their own or didnt want to because it tied them to summer after summer in the same place. What's the matter with that idea? Copyrighted!

Lesley Carol Irma and Margery write that there's all that heart could wish going on on the farm we have. We have a small horse (Morgan) we bought for a saddle horse when very young. We brought it with us at too much expense from Franconia. It has eaten its head off several times over when we have had to board it out in our absence on various errands of mercy and education in the winters. We were just beginning to resent what it had cost us when lo and behold on converting it into a driving horse we find we have a trotter. You may hear of Carol or me on the turf next.

Not that I'm losing my interest appreciably in writing as an art. I shall have another book before many years. I've scattered poems enough around in the magazines for two books if I can get up energy enough to gather them together again.

This has been a year to wonder at. I don't know what I haven't done this year. I've had no assigned work as you may have heard. I've been supposed to have nothing to do but my writing and the University has been supposed to have nothing to do with me but take credit for my writing. In practice it has turned out humorously. I've been pretty busy dining out and talking informally on all occasions from club meetings to memorial services on the athletic field on Decoration Day. I have felt non-sensical at times. But it's the first year of an experiment. We want to find out if every college couldn't keep one artist or poet and the artist or poet and college be the better for the mutual obligation. There'll be less lionizing when the thing settles down and people get used to the idea. Miami University at Oxford Ohio has undertaken Percy Mackay and Michigan University has undertaken me. That is as far as the idea has got yet. I'm probably coming back next year on a slightly modified plan. I am to be free to be clear away from the place for nine months out of the twelve. I've decided I would have to get very much done. I'll have a house here but it'll stand empty in memory of me most of the time.

Oh gee I wish I could see you as on the day I left you on the corner in Derry Village and you set off for Vancouver or on the day when I saw you with Margaret sitting on the high bank above the baseball field the year after you graduated or on the night when you turned up at my reading at Exeter or as on the day when you got punched in the eye by one of Kemp's boys from Sanborn (was his name White or Doble or what was it?) or as on the day when you got mad at me about Pamir or something in class or as on the night when you put the candles out on Doc Faustus with your finger ends and generally acted so like the Devil.

There was talk of my ranging west last winter, but I backed out. I'd go if Elinor would go with me next winter. I doubt if she will."

Even when they boosted the monthly income to four hundred dollars, they dared not ease off. Sickness was always a threat, and in the summer of 1924 John returned from a convention in Estes Park with a high fever. Just before the Fourth of July he entered the hospital with pericarditis, leaving instructions with Margaret to be sure to buy the usual supply of fireworks, even if he were sick. Grandmother Bartlett came West to help Margaret in the double task of caring for the children and keeping up the income with her articles. Margaret feared that this time John would not get well, confiding her worries in her nine- and ten-year-old sons who would have to help. It was weeks before John was home and well again.

The winter brought more illness: measles for all the children, followed by my having pneumonia. A two-year-old, I remember nothing of the illness, but Margaret often told of the all-night vigil, listening to the sound of my wheezy breath, until I awoke with a healthy holler, a sign the crisis had passed. All I know, after that winter my curly baby hair turned straight.

Margaret came through the winter close to exhaustion, and pregnant. She needed household help, and John needed stenographic help; they needed indoor plumbing and a heated house, and they needed to be closer to a doctor if he had to come on the run. They moved into Boulder, renting a brick house on Mapleton Avenue in the "less prosperous" section of town for thirty dollars a month. It was only two blocks "over the hill" to country farms, but the streetcar line ran just a block away, a civilized jangle, harsh to country-tuned ears.

We brought the chickens with us, but as a concession to "town standards" found a hermit in Sunshine Canon to keep the goats. We never publicly claimed ownership, but some years later there were stories of a herd of untended goats butting telephone poles in Sunshine Canon—descendants of Billy and Theda, no doubt.

This was the house that became the "office house." A downstairs bedroom was furnished with two desks, each with a typewriter, placed near the bay windows, and with two other large desks, forming an "L," always piled high with trade journals and manuscripts. Margaret sat behind one of the big desks, often using the pulled-out drawer for "working space" when there was none left on the desk proper. She suffered two miscarriages after moving into town, but I don't remember a day she spent in bed, a day when she wasn't in her office working by nine in the morning.

John's dictating machine was in the upstairs bedroom where Johnny and Richard had twin beds; I was in my teens before I realized the "quack, quack" played back on the cylinders was really "comma, quotes." The stenographer typed from nine to five, Margaret using her typewriter after she left until seven o'clock, when she went into the kitchen to fix supper.

Unwilling to let go of country freedom, our world as children was the barn on the back of the lot. Left over from an earlier time, it was a misbegotten structure with a loft, accessible only by ladder, horse stalls, and cellar door in the floor, which spiders tried to seal shut with dusty webs. Maybe half-a-dozen times a summer, on very sunny days, we'd dare to pull open the cellar door and descend the steps, thick with gray powdery dust, to the dank, black cellar hole. Two rooms in the barn had once been plastered and wall-papered for living quarters, dark rooms that after the hired hands moved out had been given over to chickens. The owner of the house had left an old Reo touring car parked in the barn, propped up on wood blocks; and "riding the Reo," we would find our privacy to leaf through magazines and eat green apples, hiding a salt shaker in the springs through a hole in the horsehair seats. The barn was our world. John and

Margaret never went there, and neither did we—after dark.

The change from country to town was harder on the older boys, who had to face a new school and new faces—in knickers and black stockings. To John and Margaret this was "proper dress" for school boys, whether anyone else dressed that way or not. (They didn't.) John felt he was a professional and so the children should get to know the "right sort of people," a vague sort of standard and difficult to meet since we didn't live among the professional and business people whose homes were on University Hill or Mapleton Hill. Always sensitive to criticism by neighbors, town living, for all its convenience, was a bit of a trial. A phone call— "Did you know your little girl is climbing on the roof?" —was an awful embarrassment for my mother. It seemed most anything would give rise to "what will the neighbors think!"

Forrest and Johnny, of course, were to learn early how to make their way in the world of business. Each had a *Saturday Evening Post* route, with stern lectures on "determination and success" if they returned home without selling all the magazines. "Don't be satisfied until you've made your sales," John would say. Rather than go out again on a cold winter day, and too shy to tell the dealer he didn't want so many *Posts*, Forrest would ditch his extra copies in the walls of the house, dropping them down out of sight from the opening in the unfinished second-floor attic. He paid for the copies himself out of his profits from regular subscribers. Johnny wouldn't take a loss. He'd just take as many *Posts* as he could sell.

But growing boys brought worries. Johnny, crossing

an icy street to board a streetcar that didn't stop, was hit by a car and broke his leg. Accidents can happen in any climate, but both Margaret and John, hearing Elinor's concern for Carol's health, undiagnosed but bronchial in nature, regarded themselves as living testimonials on behalf of Colorado's climate. Everyone should, they felt, try it.

Still at Ann Arbor, Frost wrote on December 11, 1925:

"We wrote to Carol at about the same time we were writing to you. At about the same time you were answering Carol apparently wasn't. Don't you get too ready to have him for Christmas company. He will be moved to act slowly if at all. He's a good boy and faithful to what he sets his hand to, which is the same as saying not unamiably obstinate. His heart is in his Vermont projects, the flower garden and the orchard. It will come hard for him to break off and start all over. He has something of my father in him that won't own up sick. It's from no ideal of gameness either. He's just naturally self-disregardful. He rather dispises frail careful people. But never mind he may listen to us in the long run. He may sooner than I expect. Anyway we had to make a beginning with him.

Well you have your children to suffer with. You know how it is. A broken leg from an automobile! It sounds like a narrow escape. I hope the leg was all.

More soon when I hear from Carol. This is just to thank you for your letter, you ould friend."

The children grew and the business grew. Margaret, relieved of housework by a girl who came daily from eight to three and prepared "dinner" at noon, merged her spare-time writing activities with John's editorial service. After the years of a one-to-one return, doing the legwork, interviewing, and then writing a single article, John established Bartlett Syndicate Service, training correspondents in all parts of the West to meet the needs of national trade magazines. Margaret sent out assignments; edited, marketed, and kept track of mountains of manuscripts each month, including John's. She always signed her name "M.A. Bartlett" or just used the initials "M.A.B." Some editors didn't know for twenty years that she was a woman.

To increase the return per word, which was still a half to one and a half cents, they thought up "The Big Eight Clip Sheet." The syndicated material was printed on newspaper-sized sheets of quality paper and all of it was written by John and Margaret Bartlett under various pen names: H. R. Simpson, A. Shaw Place (the name of the Pawtuckaway farm), and verse by Vernon Varney. Each monthly issue contained eight items, including a special business article, legal article, a feature on credit and collections, a "Bag of Advertising Tricks," and a verse or jingle. The articles were priced separately, or there might be a group fee. Sending the sheet to leading trade papers, a five-dollar article might be sold fifteen times. All the children helped with the mailings, spreading the thick pad of sheets on the floor and folding each one, stuffing envelopes, sorting, stamping, then fitting the fat envelopes into *Saturday Evening Post* bags to take to the post office.

Margaret gave up children's stories and her household articles, but her poems, which appeared in *Seed World,*

The Flower Grower, New England Homestead, and others, were her one outlet for the expression of her feelings. The view from the typewriter where she'd sit after the stenographer left was transformed into print:

To My Neighbor in Her Garden

Neighbor, from my window,
Through the summer hours,
I have watched you working
Out among your flowers.

While I've wielded pencil,
Tied to office chair,
Heart and soul have wandered
With your flowers there.

Typewriters are clicking,
But you, beneath the trees,
Change their noise to droning
Of the garden bees.

Air grows rank and heavy—
But a glance at you,
And your garden fragrance
I am breathing, too.

Black type on white paper!
How the head droops, weary,
Till your bright-hued garden
Smiles at me so cheery.

Neighbor, in your garden,
Working with your flowers,

You make song and sunshine
For my indoor hours.

Lean Mr. Jones, the mail carrier, walked the rest of his route an inch taller after unloading the magazines and stacks of business envelopes at 2005 Mapleton. Returns were coming in, though, yearly income passing the five-thousand-dollar mark, going for ten thousand. Times were good for the enterprising before 1929!

Frost was still in Michigan as a fellow in letters, but his children were "staying put" in New England. In answer to a "catching up" kind of letter from John, Frost wrote from The Open Book at 124 South Street in Pittsfield, Massachusetts, at New Year's, 1926:

"You and Margaret were my favorite kids at Pinkerton you know whether taken singly or as a pair. So it won't be anything on me particularly if you happen to come out right. I mean I won't be as sorry as—— —— for example. Mind you, though, I don't insist on success. Feel perfectly free to come out any way you please. Lose if you think it will get you in better with God. I shall still write you letters oftener than I do anyone else except my very own children.

I can answer a few of your questions. I'm doing at Ann Arbor next to nothing now. I shall have one seminar a week in writing of all kinds but hand next term. You wouldn't say I wrote much. I have done four small books in twenty-eight years, one in seven. I think the rate increases a little. I can't be sure. I have got so I answer almost no letters. Do I lecture? I talk as much as I am able to. The platform takes it out of me. One year I hurt myself. Pullman training, dining out and wagging a swallow tail behind a lecturn. This year we are limiting me to less than last year. . . .

I try not to have more than three or four on a trip. This we still feel is more than is good for me. My worst year was forty exposures. Some of the time I have needed the money but mostly I haven't. I must have told you I have had tours planned that would have taken me through Colorado. But I didn't feel up to them. I'd like well enough some excuse to visit you. I guess I'll have to visit you without an excuse some time. That's what it will come to.

I am not sure of hanging on long at Ann Arbor though the position is supposed to be for life. It's too far from the children for the stretch of our heart strings. Carol probably won't be budged. And here's Lesley and Marjorie in the book business in Pittsfield. We've just come on to be with Marj for an operation for appendicitis. She's been having bronchial pneumonia. We don't like to be scattered all over the map as long as we don't have to be. Elinor stands being separated from the children worse than I do. What I want is a farm in New England once more.

One advantage of being here is it gives me a chance at all the brand new books without money and without price. I've just read Lord Gray's Twenty-five Years (corker), Charnwood's Gospel of St. John (worth a look into if you want to know the latest higher criticism), The Pancha-tantra (the most ancient book of anecdotes, source of most now going) and Max Eastman's Since Lenin Died (in hopes of getting the truth at last from our fiercest American Communist). Gee they're all good books. Any book I can't let alone is a good book. I go months years without reading a thing. Then I read 'em at the rate of three a day. Willa Cather is our great novelist now. Her Professor's House is all right. I wonder what you would say to such an able but sordid book as Sherwood Anderson's Dark Laughter. Probably you won't find that last in your public library.

I'll try to write you a letter of ideas another time. This is all things. . . .

Eighteen below here yesterday.

Have a good year."

There was little time for reading or any leisure-time activity. John bought *Dark Laughter*—at least it was on our bookshelves—and he read *Harper's*, the *American Mercury*, and *Literary Digest*. Summers, we'd have a week or two in the mountains at Hessie, one of a group of five cabins a mile beyond the mining town of Eldora. We'd load a hired Cadillac touring car with cartons of manuscripts, the typewriter, and the children. Tied to the spare tire in the rear was a coaster wagon, an annual Christmas gift to the boys, but hardly regarded with much joy. Its main function was to transport groceries, milk, and the mail brought daily by "stage" from Eldora to Hessie. John would take time to fish for trout with the boys, occasionally catching enough for a meal, and make willow whistles that worked every time. We'd hike to the ghost town at Camp Pitts, walking the logs of a decaying corduroy road, running to take shelter from a sudden midafternoon shower in a deserted cabin or in the dampness of a mine tunnel, building a fire to dry out clothes and roast marshmallows. Margaret kept the manuscripts going out, working at night by oil lamps, listening to the boys argue whose turn it was to cross the pasture to fill the two pails with icy creek water, cooking on monkey stoves with damp wood to tease out a reluctant, smoky fire, and making a midnight trek to the outhouse before climbing into bed. On the whole, Margaret preferred her mountains for "looking at," rather than "living in." Margaret's heart, weak since childhood, began causing trouble, with severe heart pains and fluttering that prevented continuing summers at Hessie after the twenties. John would still take a week or two at Hessie or Duck Lake near Ward, accompanied by one or more of the children, while he worked on his books.

One thing both Margaret and John were sure of as parents: We should learn to deal with the world, just as they had had to do. Margaret disapproved strongly of Elinor's protective attitude toward her children, taking them out of school if they didn't like it. We went to school, just as we went to Sunday school, like soldiers dutifully marching to war, more frightened than eager, somewhat surprised to find no war going on. An out and out rash, like chicken pox, was good for a few days in bed, but colds were overlooked; and many's the time the school nurse sent one or another of us back home to be rubbed with hot camphorated oil and put to bed for another day before marching off again. Quite different was the Frosts' hovering around their children, by now in their twenties, married or seeking marriage. Margaret and John would shake their heads; "if only they'd stop *interfering!*"

Frost wrote again around May of 1926 from Ann Arbor, Michigan:

"Let's see if I can remember what all has happened since the flurry last fall about transporting Carol to Colorado for his health. I was skeptical about prying him loose from his attachments to the South Shaftsbury farm. He's getting more and more dug in there with every tree and bush he makes a hole for. Right now he is adding a hundred Astrachan trees to the dwarf orchard—dwarf so as to get them sooner for the roadside market. He's putting in some sixty of Miss White's (of Whitesbog N J.) cultivated high-bush blueberries. And a lot of roses. The process is the dragnet process. You try everything and throw away what you don't like. He and Lillian [Carol's wife] sold a hundred dollars worth of sweet peas last summer with a small hand printed sign. There's a new girls college just starting at Bennington four miles away on which he builds some hope of a more or less flowery kind of farming. It may come to a hot house in the end. And it may not. He lost one of his great big workhouses a week or so ago. Farming has hard setbacks. In that loss went about all he had earned in teaming in the woods all winter. He's such a worker as I was never suspected of being though I may have been: so don't be too ready to grin your low-minded Rockingham County Mephistophules. . . .

We're going east again said the pendulum. This was no go this year, or rather it was too much go and what wasn't go was come. Marjorie's long illness (means more than sickness) kept Elinor with her in Pittsfield Mass and me commuting for months. Every week or so I would run the water out of the pipes and leave the house here to freeze. It wasnt exactly in the contract to try to keep it up here with the children back there and such things likely to happen again. And anyway I want a farm. It's all arranged so you needn't exclaim a protest about such whiffling. Amherst, Dartmouth, Bowdoin and Connecticut Wesleyan are going to give me a living next year for a couple of weeks in each of them. The rest of the time I shall be clear away from the academic, feeding pigeons hens dogs or anything you advise for the pleasure or profit in it. The only thing that worries me is that Bennington college coming in on our pastoral serenity. I ran away from two colleges in succession once and they took revenge by flattering me back to teach in college. Now I am running away again and it looks as if they would come after me. I'll probably end with one of the ponderous things in bed with me on my chest like an incubus. Look out or the same fate will overtake you, or so I begin to fear from what you tell me about the friendliness of your University out there. We may both live to be sorry we didn't go through school in the regular course of nature and get it over with.

You've got adopted and adapted there. But me, I'm sort of a Yankee from New England. I want to get back, if its just the same to everybody. Nothing's invidious about my preference. I like Michigan people and I like Michigan. Only only."

John spent the next year, 1927, working on his first book, *Retail Credit Practice*, finally retreating to the old Columbia Hotel in Ward, Colorado, to finish the final manuscript free from interruption. Margaret had suffered several months of severe rheumatism during the winter, her arms and fingers stiffening to wood each night. In the morning she'd have John stand her upright, like a doll being set in motion for the day. She'd force her arm to do her bidding, painfully raising the hairbrush to smooth her hair, determined to make her fingers weave the braids and set the hairpins tight. By noon she'd have limbered her fingers on the typewriter, and she'd work late into the night, putting off going to bed where her joints would stiffen in her sleep. The trouble was eventually traced to abscessed teeth. When her teeth were pulled, Margaret turned her back to us, or held her hand over her mouth, not wanting to be seen, waiting to get the new dentures within a week "so the gums won't shrink." She never took her teeth out at night, either, once her dentures were fitted. After the rheumatism went away, Margaret began to put on weight, and for the first time in her life became rounded and "matronly" in figure.

John's sickness that year was a bout of winter grippe, but he found time to write a lengthy letter to Gorham Munson who was writing a biography of Frost. "I haven't written it with the thought you will want to make much use of it—but, surely, a biographer of Robert Frost should have before him information from Rob's closest friend." He apparently sent off a note to Frost, brief because of illness. The reply came from South Shaftsbury on November 1, 1927:

"You must be terribly sick. I see you the way you were beside the store that summer night on Patuckaway Mountain. You have a right to be sick if you want to. We haven't all got to be healthy. I refuse to be tyrranized

over by doctors. But I don't want you terribly or danger-
ously sick, Captain. I started cringeing at the way you
played yourself ragged in the fall and slopped round on
wet feet all that last winter in Derry and you have kept
me cringeing more or less ever since. Well, what's the
use of talking.

I wish it was Elinor and I seeing you about now instead
of them two irresponsible wastrels our son and daughter
[Carol and Lillian] hell bent for California. I sometimes
come within an ace of taking up with invitations out that
way. What decides me against it is the family. I can't
leave them for more than a day or two. If they ever get
so they will consent to follow me across the prairies, the
first place I'll lead them to will be Boulder. Then we will
have a good old talk as in the days that were.

Carol is a curious boy. I wonder if this expedition of
his is to spy out a new country to live in. He wouldn't say
so if it was and it may not be. He'll have told you he is
pretty deeply involved here what with his considerable
sweet pea business and his MacIntosh apples in prospect.

I've been playing myself out back in the bog in his
absence throwing wheelbarrow after wheelbarrows full
of stones off the wall into the mud and peat to rebuild the
old causeway to the back pasture. We've been having
days I doubt if you could beat in Colorado: the air at a
standstill, the leaf gold still holding out on the trees, frost
just barely some nights, others none. Me for it. But it
can't last or I can't—I've got to go down to see a President inaugurated at Amherst day after tomorrow. (I
ought not to complain. He is somewhat of my choosing.)
I'll have to look up my shoes and see if my clothes have
improved any by not having been worn lately. A dip

in kerosene coal oil will start the rust. Then I can holley-stone it off.

The first report I have had on the biographical sketch speaks chiefly of your contribution to it. I aint agoing to thank you. It was an inspiration of mine to give Munson direct access to my past through two or three of my independent friends. I thought it would be fun to take the risk of his hearing something to my discredit. The worst you could [reveal] was my Indian vindictiveness. Really I am awful there. I am worse than you know. I can never seem to forgive people that scare me within an inch of my life. I am going to try to be good and cease from strife. . . .

My isn't it a chill to hear how those youngsters of yours are coming up? If they are that old how old must I be? Tell them easy does it. They must be fine children who can be appealed to. You can't so much as grow in this world without affecting somebody to tears. People had better be careful how they grow. There is something invidious about the way the young grow. I'd like to tease them. They look as if they could take care of themselves. I probably couldnt baffle them very much at my crypticest. Never mind I can baffle some people."

John's book, to be published in the fall of 1928, was accepted by Harper's in New York, an accomplishment that was the culmination of his work and experience in the field of research and business analysis. Income had reached nearly ten thousand dollars for the year; they were going to act a little rich and buy a car. It was a blue 1928 Essex sedan, and John's first thought was to take a triumphant trip back to New England, returning in glory, so to speak, the successful son come home. Frost, in South Shaftsbury, was duly warned, and wrote in June of 1928:

"Hooray! To think that I shall set eyes on you in twenty days!—you and the only other Pinkerton graduate I ever really thought worth an A. It's longer since I saw her than since I saw you. The last time I saw you, I guess, you were disappearing on foot down the wrong side of the hill into Littleton New Hampshire. That must be ten years ago—one tenth of a lifetime, to put it mildly. The trouble is you won't stay round long enough. The minute you get here you'll begin to threaten to leave for Raymond. Them's Elinor's sentiments and Carol and Lillian's too. Gee why can't you put the Bartlett Service on the running board if there isn't room for it in the car with the four children and transplant it to the east. It ought not to be too old to transplant. And any way they transplant trees of almost any age now.

Come on!"

Margaret stayed up until 4:00 A.M. getting the Bartlett Syndicate Service caught up and ahead; the Essex was loaded down with sleeping bags on each front fender and camping gear (tent and stove) on the running board. One night of pitching the tent and cooking by camp stove was enough to exhaust the delights of "camping out." We stayed in cottage camps, the tiny early day motels, which were often, according to Johnny who seemed to feel he slept in the sleeping bag on the floor more often than anybody, "made over chicken coops." John, totally a sincere man himself, was sometimes taken

146

in by advertising claims, and had filled the car with oil "guaranteed to last two thousand miles." At gas stations he'd say with confidence, "don't bother to check the oil," until we burned out a bearing.

Forrest, fourteen, with an inborn knowledge of mechanics, did much of the driving, sitting on a cushion in order to see over the hood. John never mastered the art of releasing the clutch. "Whoops, here!" he'd say, always surprised by the jerk that would send my head against the dashboard.

The Beautiful Missouri looked muddy; in Gettysburg it poured rain; I was carsick regularly, twice a day, and sat on the front seat on Margaret's lap for miles and miles, breathing hot dusty air and engine fumes seeping through the floor boards, until I'd shout "Stop!" and try to choke back the returning meal. The brief walk beside the road was never long enough; and Margaret's heart bothered her. "John, you're driving too fast!" she'd say when the gauge registered 35 m.p.h. It was a long trip.

To the children, relatives and friends were a blur of many faces, except Grampa Abbott who showed us a "real Fourth," holding the firecrackers in his hand as the fuse burned way down and casually tossing them, chuckling as they'd explode in the air. We felt we saw everybody in the state of New Hampshire, but we were shy with people. Fireflies; piles of wooden heels, cast-offs from a shoe factory; stone walls and ponds; tent caterpillars and "old John," the "retired tramp" who stayed at Grammie Bartlett's—these were the things to remember.

Visiting the Frosts' in South Shaftsbury, Vermont, we went with Carol, Lillian, and their son, Prescott, to

147

look at a cave; but except for Forrest, who liked to hunt for fossils, arrowheads, and was interested in such things, the rest of us scrambled right out into the warmth of the sunlight. We'd seen the movie *Huckleberry Finn* on the way East, the first movie I'd ever seen, and had been so thoroughly frightened by the cave I had no interest in really being caught in one. Prescott, Lillian, and I hunted for wild strawberries instead. Carol took Forrest for an astonishing hell-bent ride in his Model T Ford over the dirt farm road, making a tremendous stir of dust for such a soft-spoken, gentle man.

Johnny was treated to a ride into town with John and Rob to get an ice-cream soda, memorable because John, whose attention when driving was on talk, not road signs, started the wrong way up a one-way street. He'd shifted into reverse when a shiny Buick with New York license plates pulled alongside, with a nattily dressed driver at the wheel. "What do you think you're doing?" he asked, flashing his gold teeth. "Who are you?" answered Frost, glaring. "You're going the wrong way," the stranger answered, still baring his gold teeth. "*Who are you? Please introduce yourself before you speak to us!*"

Deciding he'd backed up against the wrong man, the Buick-driver took off, with Frost saying after him, "And the next time you see a stranger in town, be as *rude* as you can."

For the next ten minutes, driving back to the farm, Frost filled the car with such earthy oratory as "absolute jackass," and "absolute s-o-b." Johnny thoroughly enjoyed the display of rough talk, for in our house "gee whiz" and "gosh" were the extent of allowed expressions. Anyone who could use such language must be all right, young Johnny felt, even if he did write poetry. Possibly on the strength of his new regard for Frost, Johnny tried swinging birches, "but with poor results."

John enjoyed every minute of the visit, talking with Pinkerton teachers and Raymond people. He indulged in reliving some of his boyhood, shooing the family to the other side of a pond so he could take a swim in the raw.

When we finally reached Boulder again, after two months of feeling adrift on an endless expanse of land, I walked in the familiar yard and touched the roses that had come into bloom by the front step, the peony with its too-heavy blossom, and climbed to the top of the apple tree. The next morning the typewriters beat out the rhythm of home; and we sought the welcome privacy of the barn to eat hard green apples, regretting only that Colorado didn't have fireflies.

In the fall John's book was published, and in its limited circle of interest was a moderate success. Mostly, its benefits were not in direct sales as much as in prestige. He was an "authority," a professional, henceforth, in business matters. Although he never sent Rob magazines containing his articles, he now sent the book, along with a review he'd done of Frost's new book, *West-running Brook*.

In the winter of 1928, Rob wrote:

"You did that just right—I mean with just the right admixture of the personal you and me. It should have been different from any other review I ever had and it was different. You brought it off with perfect discretion. I might have dreaded it from anyone else I ever raised by hand. I knew you could be trusted to flatter me un-sentimentally—you old hard-head. Them sentences have to say what you tell them to. You're an expert. That is obvious in your book which I have read at and read a good deal of since it came—much to my enlightenment in the ways of the business world. I ought to review you now to even things up. Give me time to turn reviewer.

This is a short letter. I'm back at Amherst on the job of doing not much but sit round talking educational philosophy as distinguished from pedagogy. I'll surely have to come out there some day and see more of you. We didn't half talk it over when you were here."

With one book to his credit, John felt again the rest-lessness of spirit that sought satisfaction in "something new."

For the first time since 1912 he invested some money in a publication, and became managing editor and co-publisher of *The Author and Journalist* magazine in Denver. Riding high with the times, he bought some Poland Bonds, watching for the newspaper every evening to check the quotations which climbed higher and higher, dropping a little, then rising. One day they dropped to nothing. The Poland Bonds were hidden in the drawer, never to be mentioned in polite conversation again.

But not to be dismayed, John held great faith in the basic soundness of American business. In 1929, attending a meeting of the National Association of Business Writ-ers, of which he was permanent secretary, he issued a statement of hope and promise; as he remarked later, "We were wrong, like everybody else."

VI

Colorado Visits,
1930-1934

IN THE thirties John's interests branched out in different directions, partly because of the depression, which cut the Syndicate's markets in half, and partly due to his inner restlessness. Achieving professional status with his book, he lost interest in the personal interview, saying "the bang went out of it." Margaret was handling Bartlett Syndicate Service, and just "armchair" writing was not enough for John. He bought the Boulder *Daily Doings*, an advertising publication for local merchants, published weekly during the tourist-summer school season, and the quarterly *Mountain States Hardware and Implement Association* magazine. Both were small enterprises, run mostly on advertising, but good money-makers for the amount of time required to publish them. He entered local organizations: the Rotary Club, Town and Gown, the Chamber of Commerce, eventually serving each group as president, with the usual committee work and holding of minor offices. His alliance with the University of Colorado was never close; there was mostly a professional friendship with faculty members whom he knew through organizations.

In 1930, however, the University of Colorado instituted the Rocky Mountain Writer's Conference, and John tried to lure Rob out, hoping for a visit. Rob's reply was from Franconia, dated in the summer of that year:

"I'd like the engagement at your writer's institute as an excuse to visit you. But I don't know about pulling out at that time of year and taking Elinor to the altitude of one mile for any length of time. That would have to be honestly enquired into. I dont suppose Colorado is specially recommended for the weak of heart. We're not the strength we were, you have to remember, and can't do all sorts of things the way we used to.

If we decide I ought to come, I'll do it for anything you say, but if its left to me to say, really for my self respect I should ask for rather more than $600. I say self-respect when I mean the public respect. It is a miserable business being a poet among professors and business men. The only way to make them respect you is to make them pay.

We're off here in Franconia (altitude of house site 1700 ft.) for my nose more as a matter of form than necessity for I seem to have lost my nose for hay fever. At least we think I have. Next year we may stay in the lowlands to find out for sure. It would make a great difference in our outlook.

Marj is in hospital in Baltimore where she lay a hopeless invalid two years ago, now training to be a nurse. Lesley is in New York with her husband and her baby. Carol is farming at the stone house where you saw him. Irma is going to college at Mass Agricultural College next year with her husband and her baby. Her husband has been farming near us but is turning to landscape architecture so-called. We have three grand children in three different families. One of the grand children starts school this year and so begins again the endless round. The first school I went to at his age was in San Francisco along about fifteen years after the Civil War (We're almost that far from the World War) I cried (wept) myself out of that first school in one day not because the teacher was a negress (which she was) but on general principles. I didn't get back again for two years. I've been jumping school ever since."

The plans for the Writer's Conference were worked out, and possibly Frost's commitment to come to Boulder in the summer of 1931 made it reasonable to send Marjorie to us. Her nurse's training had been interrupted with illness, diagnosed as TB, which to Margaret meant only one thing: Marjorie *must* come to Colorado. They prevailed on the Frosts, and in the early spring Johnny drove the old Essex to the train depot to meet Marjorie and take her to the Mesa Vista TB Sanitarium on the hill just three blocks from our house. Rob wrote in the spring of 1932:

"Marjorie wrote in her last letter, Don't say our family never does anything right. In her opinion we did a big thing right when we sent her out where the John T. Bartletts live. I don't know that she says right out, but she seems to imply, that she doesn't think much of your Colorado spring as far as it has got. But that defect sinks into a joke by comparison with all she does think much of. Between you and me (you mustn't tell her for fear of making her self-conscious) you folks and Colorado have changed her tune. You know where to come for thanks if you want any in words.

She wants me to come out there and do the cooking for the sanatorium she intends to establish when she gets well and finishes training for a nurse. She says I am a good meat cook—that's where I would come in. Elinor could do the bread and pastry. Carol could run the dairy and kitchen garden. What dissipates that dream is your altitude. You live too high for us—about 2500 feet too high. Cut your plateau down half and we'll talk with you. Why can't you be reasonable? Twenty five hundred up ought to be enough for anybody who began life on the plains of Raymond, New Hampshire. Come down I won't say off it—come down with it. Shake down, have an earthquake. I mean it. I'd like to live out there for a few years if it were only possible. We are not wedded to this state. For some funny reason we have never been accepted as Vermonters. We are important enough to have the question raised whether or not we should be accepted. We were that flattered. But the answer has been in the negative. So we can go when and where we please. Well we'll have some farms to sell when we mobilize. Three. Mine of 1500 acres a hewn timber house with three open fireplaces on the central chimney and many HL hinges on the doors. Carol's of 100 acres and the stone house you remember; very old and historical. John and Irma's of 8 acres and a small old house in a half circle of old spruces. Allow me to sell you a couple. Don't weep for us. I can unload them if I turn my hand to advertising. Give me a year.

We mustn't think so far ahead. It will be something to have a few weeks out there with you this summer. We'll want to be sure of Elinor of course. But if the doctors give her permission, I don't see why we shouldn't all have a gay time together.

I'm studying the catalogue of the Summer School so I shall be up on my fellows on the faculty. I ought to have read what they have written when I meet them. Yes and they ought to have read what I have written. But will they have? I ask you. Once in a while I meet someone who has read me. It did him good. I mean it served him right.

This is the time of year that I have been keeping away from my farm things all winter for. Now I am let loose to go the rounds of them all to see how they came through. I didn't winter-kill (though I damn near did in one of those New York hotels). Did they winter kill? A few blew down and a few spruces dried up in the big wind of March 9. But most things stood it and are ready [to] start their new growth. I've got the trellis of a grape-vine to rebuild.

People aren't kind to me about my farming any more.

They make jokes like the one I had to listen to today. A friend says to me says he: You look poorly for you. You've had too much city. After you've sat down on your farm for a few months you'll be as good as new. I have to admit that I don't work at anything profitable like milking or pitching down hay. I move trees around the way Amphron did only he did it by music proper and I do it by hand."

Marjorie Frost was the only friend the family ever shared. Except for her, we each had our separate friends and relationships, with almost no overlapping of interest. Margaret and John rarely saw or spoke with neighbors, the "Grandma's" I adopted, and spent many hours visiting in their kitchens and gardens as they worked. The families of the children "around the block" with whom we'd play kick-the-can and Red Light never came to call, nor did my mother know them, even by sight, for she rarely walked outside in the yard except to brush snow off the ash pit to leave suet and crumbs for the birds in the winter. She never went shopping. Groceries were delivered, as was the laundry, and the children ran errands downtown. By the time I was in second grade, what couldn't be bought by mail order I would select myself in the stores and bring home "on approval." It was something new to have Margaret hustle through her supper dishes and be driven to the sanitarium in the evening for a visit with Marjorie.

Johnny owned a Model T Ford, bought with his own money and permitted only on the condition that he go out for football for one season. Dad could never understand how none of his boys showed any interest in sports, especially Johnny, who was so husky and generally belligerent. Johnny warmed the bench for the season, hated the whole foolish business of tiring yourself out over a ball, but bought his Model T. He'd occasionally take Marjorie for rides in the afternoon, and either Johnny or one of his cronies would play chess with her.

We never thought of Marjorie as sick or had any fear of TB. It was simply a dreadful disease in New England that the Colorado climate would cure. I tagged along once in a while in the evening, but the memories of my own visits are not a part of the real world of people. I remember Marjorie best framed against a hospital pillow, her dark hair brushed pompadour style away from a cameo-tinted face, her finely sculptured features and enchanting dark eyes. She bore no relation to anyone associated with my everyday world or my business-house home; she seemed a part of the world of fairy tales I'd read about under my covers by flashlight at night. Visiting her after school was a pilgrimage to a princess in a castle, rather than a sick call. I'd hide my roller skates in the bushes at the bottom of the steep, broad sidewalk leading to the main hospital building and approach the front door with considerable fright, for the giant shade trees on the lawn and shadowing the front entrance made a completely different atmosphere than that of the arid, sunny hill on which the sanitarium was built. I suppose we talked, but mostly I remember how Marjorie looked, and the guilty but wonderful secret of having peeked in a cardboard box of her belongings in our attic and of finding an exotic raspberry red silk shawl with a nine-inch fringe there. Only a fairy-tale ball would have been a splendid enough occasion for such finery!

Rob and Elinor tried our climate that summer, staying as guests in our house, a situation we'd never met before. To make room, Johnny and his dog, Caesar, slept in the barn. Johnny, seven years older than I, was the tease, the bully of my childhood, against whom I was forever pitting my temper unmatched by strength. I invested him with very few generous or heroic qualities, but his overnight sleep in the spooky barn (I always ran past it after dark; its black windows held back frightful secrets.) was a deed to inspire awe and admiration. Guests important enough to require such heroism on his part probably made me run in fright. I kept a safe distance.

Rob gave Johnny a five-dollar tip for chauffering him to the sanitarium in his Model T. My brother used the money to take a ride in a barnstorming airplane, but he never told the family of his adventure until he was a grown man with children of his own.

Nothing else remains of this visit except the remark Rob made about Forrest, who was to enter the University in the fall: "Aren't you afraid of sending your boys to college? Aren't you fearful what it might do to them?"

We were more fearful of what would happen if we didn't go. John and Margaret were acutely sensitive of not having college degrees, living in a university town. They were as sure that we should go to college as that we should have shoes and bread.

And the cost of shoes and bread and coal and secretarial help was the most frequent topic of dinner-table conversation. Actually, we did not fare badly during the depression, in comparison with other families on the block. There were families on relief, and several of my playmates, I'm sure, never tasted butter except for the butter on crackers I'd serve them after school. It was a source of pride to Margaret that we were never reduced to eating oleomargarine. We still had steak and roasts, and all through the winter we'd have apples by the bushel basket. Christmas was unbearably exciting, with an orange in the toe of each stocking; and one year Richard's first pair of long pants (a concession to the dress of the day made earlier than the older boys had enjoyed) were somehow rolled tightly and squeezed into his stocking to make it look like a giant sausage. On the Fourth of July it was traditional that we'd invite all our friends on the block to come after dark to help shoot off a bountiful supply of skyrockets, Roman candles and sparklers, and set the pinwheels whirring red and blue sparks against the maple tree in the front yard.

Increasingly, in the thirties, as I grew old enough to become aware of adult conversation, politics and matters of tax and legislation were topics of discussion. John's concern was partly an outgrowth of his writing, but at the table we felt it more in terms of the government, which seemed about to whisk the food off our plates. Rob did not share John's conservative Republican views, but they enjoyed political discussion. In the fall of 1931 Rob wrote from South Shaftsbury:

"The enclosed picture of Cal [Coolidge] in his smock and boots ought to make you more of an American if not a New Englander. There is something so touching in seeing a Republican try to pose as a Democrat. Signs like this (pretenses and poses) tell us that the Bolsheviki are coming; the reality has gone out of the old order we grew up in and gave our hearts to. But never mind; we're not politicians: we don't care too much. It isn't as if we had signed the Declaration and voted for the Constitution. It's no frame up of ours. Let it all go to pieces. There's still the comparative climate of Vermont Colorado and California to think of."

As John's time was taken up more and more by work on another book, committee responsibilities with the Rotary Club and the Chamber of Commerce, the routine jobs to keep the business going fell to Margaret. While she was fixing the supper of leftovers she'd talk to me in the kitchen, reminiscing about the Pinkerton days, the excitement of her love for John, the quickening of her pulse even now when he'd come home from a day in Denver. Forrest was dating a "steady," and the importance of the Right Love, as in her feelings for John, was told over and over again. Hers was a marriage "made in heaven," or as she expressed it in her poem called "Marriage":

> God blew two bubbles—
> Your soul and mine;
> They came together
> By plan divine;
> No longer two,
> But merged as one;
> Thus my life and your life
> As one was begun.

She believed implicitly in the Right One, and felt torn in her feelings that Forrest's girl, though very attractive, was not college educated, not of a professional family. She was *for* love, but . . . !

My brothers recall that Marjorie, who was twenty-seven in the spring of 1932, had a romantic crush on one of her doctors, and fled the sanitarium to take a room at the Boulderado Hotel one night when it had become evident the feelings were all on her side. Margaret spent a late evening with her in the hotel room, fearful of leaving Marjorie alone with her emotions in such a turmoil. Love was a starry, certain experience to Margaret, and she must have comforted Marjorie's heartache as if it were her own and convinced Marjorie that "it wasn't meant to be."

The episode passed, and Willard Fraser, a fraternity brother of Forrest's, began visiting Marjorie. Willard was a slightly built, pink-cheeked college boy, nervous but with a quick, charming smile and a soft voice. His reputation in the fraternity was somewhat that of a ladies' man, who managed to sweet-talk popular sorority girls into having dates with him. Margaret and John worried as Marjorie showed a serious interest. True love, they felt, was a pretty instantaneous thing, and Willard, for a time, kept up his social life with the sorority girls while seeing Marjorie. Margaret suffered the pangs of young love along with Marjorie, rejoicing with her when the engagement to Willard was announced.

Marjorie and Willard drove to Denver with the Bartletts to meet Rob and Elinor when they arrived for the Writer's Conference lectures in the summer of 1932. This time the Frost's stayed at the Boulderado Hotel, where Marjorie had also taken a room so that they could see more of each other. Beginning with this visit, John kept a record of conversations with Rob, writing down in hastily scribbled longhand every detail he could pull out of his memory.

The subjects ranged, as in their early years, over every kind of topic: Rob's recounting of his Derry years (quoted earlier) to talk of present affairs. Catching sight of John's newly published book, *Credit Department Salesmanship*, Rob remarked: "The honorable John hasn't sent me an inscribed copy of that book."

Of reading books and newspapers in general, Rob went on to say: "People make a vice of reading and never learn to face reality; better to read little and read well." Discussing newspaper columnists, John's opinion was: "There's more insincerity in the writer who forever attacks existing institutions than those who write supporting them." "It is logical," Frost agreed. "Our institutions grow out of ourselves. There must be much of right in them."

A surprising event was Frost's suggestion that they all attend a lecture on modern art and e.e. cummings to be given at the Little Theater on the University of Colorado campus. Frost had never been one to attend public lectures. The guest lecturer, Dr. L. W. Payne from Texas, had been a supporter of Frost's poetry in the South, and had helped him when he'd toured Texas the year before. Rob told us the story of boarding a train about three o'clock in the morning; Dr. Payne, who was seeing him off, had rushed to a fruit stand and bought a bag of pears which he thrust impulsively into Frost's hands. Rob thought he ought to go to the lecture.

"It was queer," John wrote, "to be sitting beside Frost. His face remained impassive, a little flushed, and his body tense as he followed the lecture closely." The theme was tolerance for experimental forms which indicate "progress in art." It turned out to be quite a humorous affair; Dr. Payne talking rapidly, reading cummings, and attempting in his nervous Southern accent to imitate three drunkards and an old maid. In a hasty windup after many slides and amusing, if not enlightening, comments about modern art in general, he used a more conventional cummings poem to illustrate the "true poetic feeling" possible in the new forms, "reaching the heights of Keats."

John, Margaret, Marjorie, and Willard waited in the car for Rob, who had left them somewhat nervously to go backstage to speak to Dr. Payne. When he joined them in the car he sounded off his disappointment in his friend who was "fooling around with such stuff. Comparing cummings to Keats! Keats is hard, clear; cummings is weak, sentimental, nothing else!" He didn't like the covert allusion to "questionable" material in cummings. "Probably just enough to send people hunting up his books." As the conversation moved on to talk of modern art, the tension eased. Frost could agree there was some genuine accomplishment in modern art . . . "The difficulty is in deciding when there is sincerity, or when the painter is simply laughing up his sleeve at the public."

Rob's nervousness of the evening passed. He talked of friends he'd made in Colorado the previous year, people he'd liked. There was Tom Ferril, a young poet; Morrison Shaffroth, an officer in the war, now an attorney and political figure; and young Robert Lamont, a rich man's son who had tried wheat farming and then gone into cattle ranching. Lamont had recently been to Russia "to look things over," and Rob was anxious to get his first-hand impressions and facts about the Soviet Union. Rob mused that in his early years he was restless of friendships, liking or disliking without regard for material considerations. "I am more calculating now . . . but not for myself, for my children. I think of the use that a person may sometime be to them; they may need him."

On their way to a luncheon, before leaving Boulder, Rob abruptly remembered he hadn't called at The Printed Page, Boulder's one downtown bookstore. Going into the store, he restlessly leafed through several volumes, selecting first a book on Rocky Mountain wild flowers, then changing his mind while this was being wrapped in favor of a book on Mayan culture, which caught his eye. Noticing John's nervousness about being pressed for time, Rob explained half-apologetically, "I wanted to do something for the store. Book people are having a hard time; hundreds of good book shops are going bankrupt."

It was only a four-day visit, but distressing situations were at a minimum. The Frosts went on out to Monrovia for the remainder of the summer, visiting with Carol and Lillian; Marjorie joined them there, and I never saw her again. In the fall, on their return East, Rob and Elinor stopped again in Boulder for a lecture and a few days' visit.

This visit in particular was full of irritations and annoyances, with much talk and discussion about "embarrassing situations." Rob had been misquoted by newspaper reporters, dinners were planned without his knowledge; he was asked to recite one poem to a group and then listen to somebody's "essay," giving an appreciation which he didn't think much of. Plans to meet the Lamonts required extensive discussion, with Elinor and Rob weighing this side and that, talking for an hour before finally arriving at a decision. Contrary to instructions, tickets had been sold to a dinner preceding Rob's scheduled lecture in Omaha. Should he risk an audience "freezing up" because he didn't appear at the dinner, or go to the dinner and risk being too exhausted to talk? The freedom of his conversation was watched over by Elinor, who would say, "Don't Robert!" if she thought his comment improper. (*He* didn't.)

They stayed again at the Boulderado Hotel, an eight-block walk on shaded streets from the Bartlett house. During an evening in which they pondered the ethics of existence, Rob walked home with John; John walked back to the hotel with Rob; and Rob again walked John home. "The most amazing thing to me," Rob said, "is the ability of an individual to establish a mental equilibrium before the millions of other human beings." They talked about the adjustments of children: Carol and Lillian in California, Marjorie about to be married; and for John, one youngster in college, another approaching it, but doing marginal work scholastically, not putting his mind to good use. "I can look back, and probably you can too," Rob said to John, "and see times when it seems a miracle that we 'came through.' Will has something to do with it, making the choice: run away in cowardice, or go on."

To break loose from these commitments, John and Margaret took Rob and Elinor on an afternoon's drive into the mountains, up the winding road with hairpin curves, past Nederland to Rollinsville and on to Central

City. It had once come close to being the state capital in the days of rich mining strikes, a raucously lavish boom town; but now it was a remnant recently brought to an echo of its former life by Denver artists who sponsored operas and plays in the patched up opera house in the summer. John thoroughly enjoyed showing off his mountains, inevitably scaring his passengers into clutching their seats as he'd take a hand off the wheel to point out the continental divide, the Moffat Tunnel, or the old mines which scarred the hillsides. At Blackhawk they stopped to talk to an old codger with a dark red beard, who was trying to wash out gold from soil and rock long since put through the mill. He answered their questions intelligently and conceded that placer mining made little better than a living. "It does give you an occupation," Rob commented. "Sometimes that's all it does give, an occupation," the miner answered.

From time to time Rob would point out farm buildings, the meadows of a mountain ranch, and look appraisingly. "That would make a nice place to live . . . we could probably buy that." He mentioned he was turning over in his mind the possibility of a sheep ranch for Carol. "But I don't know. Maybe I'm foolish to be thinking of it. Carol seemed to like the idea, but I don't know how much is for himself, and how much is because I'm urging him to it."

John already had another book in mind. How about Rob?

The reply was doubtful and seemed to reflect a low mood. "I've already had my *Collected Poems* published, and what does that mean if not all of them? Why go on and write poems, obscure what has already been done.

Too many writers bury themselves in the rubbish of their old age. Any prolific writer runs the risk of becoming 'common' and 'popular'. . . . Critics like to think of a 'poet's poet.' I can see some of them are already wavering . . . I'm getting too popular for them." But he had other ideas, something different, perhaps—pieces of dialogue scattered through the years in lectures. Noticing the boulders along the shore at the north end of Nederland lake—"Something like those rocks," he said, finding his way from one to another across the low land to reach the water. Maybe he'd arrive at a book.

"Why don't you write fiction and make as much as the other fellow does?" he asked John.

"Business interests me," John answered. "It's something I can do and like doing, a matter of straight thinking and getting an idea across." He pointed to the accomplishment of having his book published by Harper's on its own merits, with no professional degree or pull.

Rob didn't believe straight thinking appealed much to that crowd, but of success: "I'd rather you'd gotten something up and put it through than have a story or two published and waited around unsuccessfully the rest of your life."

Later, gathered in the hotel room, they discussed advertising. Rob's attitude was quizzical, semi-contemptuous; in general, advertising was offensive to him. Elinor smoked Chesterfields (which Rob referred to as "Chestertons"), and he thought their advertising in better taste than most. "It's not a matter of taste," John pointed out. "It is a matter of selling a product." He went on to enlarge his views to include taste, which he felt had improved from the times when advertising was restricted to the grandiose claims of the hawker, the medicine-show man, and the patent-medicine blurbs. John concluded his argument, "The trend in advertising is definitely upward."

Rob was unconvinced. "I can only see advertising leading down and down. The advertising man writes of something he knows nothing about. Like the young man I know who wrote mining promotion for an enterprise he'd never seen in Canada. When it was found out there was no development at the site, that it was all under water, the man was made a victim, embarrassed in public, and humiliated by a prison sentence. No, accuracy in writing is in inverse ratio to the distance of the writer from his subject."

The conversation was interrupted by a large wasp, winging its way into the room with a wild buzzing, distracting the attention of everyone. Rob followed it with a folded paper until it alighted on a fold in the bedspread. Making the paper into a shallow trough, he scooped up the wasp, and, carefully raising the window, gave the insect its liberty.

The Frosts departed, worrying about the Omaha lecture. In June of the following year Marjorie was married to Willard in Billings, Montana. Franklin D. Roosevelt was elected president, which overshadowed most every event for the year, as far as I could tell from dinner talk. Marjorie's marriage was not discussed as much as the phenomenon of Willard, who went directly from college into politics, a part of "that New Deal Wheeler Machine." It was not so much criticism of Willard as the system (Democratic) which encouraged young men in such a direction. Rob, reviewing the events of the year, wrote from Amherst on December 5, 1933:

"You've got some towns out there in Colorado that I surely like to inhabit mentally when I'm awake at night or out walking: and the names of them are Boulder, Larkspur, Gunnison and Crested Butte. The two best are Boulder and Gunnison. I didn't get enough of either. I believe some time I would inhabit one of them more than mentally if I weren't afraid of their altitude for Low-landers of Elinor and my age—comparative lowlanders. Our mountains leave off at five or six thousand where yours begin and our base stations where we are used to breathe are at eight hundred or a thousand. The doctors seemed to me evasive on the subject of the danger. They probably want to know more than they do about it and would be willing to have us experiment for them. I certainly felt feeble the first time I exerted myself as at Greeley and Denver and I never got over the tendency to gasp once or twice every so often day or night awake or asleep. It really makes me sorry for now that we are all in such an uprooted state of affairs something might easily come of my liking for the Rockies but for the one thing. I think Carol liked parts of Colorado better than anything outside of New England. He has no intention of staying in California. Farming there is too utterly dif-ferent from what he has grown up to. You have heard, haven't you, that Lillian is pronounced a cured person. After two years or rather a year and a half flat on her back down herself and her lung down the doctor has her on her feet and her lung restored. It's something of a miracle because Dr. Pottinger the big operator and authority out there wouldn't undertake her with her large adhesion. It's only a matter of months now when they will be free to decide for themselves whether they will risk it back in Vermont again on the same old farm. Their hearts seem set on it and particularly on the orchard of a thousand apple trees MacIntosh, Northern Spy, Golden Delicious, Red Delicious and Red Astrachan, just this year in first crop to count. I can understand their feelings but I question their wisdom. There I go again trying to run other people's lives. I must question my own wisdom. Too bad I'm not where I can govern the country as a diversion from governing my friends neighbors and relatives. (What a picture I paint of myself. I can rely on you as my partizan from of old to defend me from myself.)

I'm back at Amherst doing very little as yet but picking up the politics of the place. My feller poeticism from the Old South has improved his position with us by chivalrously punching the village policeman on the chin for illegally asking a lady what she had done with five dollars entrusted to her as local representative of the Travellers Aid. I don't much take either side. You remember how the mob started to tear Cinna to pieces for conspiracy and when told by him it was a mistake of identity, he wasn't Cinna the conspirator; he was Cinna the poet, they cried Tear him for his verses. I say it as shouldn't say it. My early detaching of myself twice over from colleges when young leaves me with a certain detachment in viewing their troubles now I am old.

I shall soon be out with a ponderous book of one poem on how I detached myself from the mills of Man in Lawrence Mass but without prejudice to machinery industry or an industrial age so that there will be no mistake in the record. I'll send you a copy. What are *you* publishing?

You want to be careful what you say to me in reply about this Democratic Nation and the Democratic Policies for the Salvation of the Soul because I have allied myself by marriage, with one of the most interesting if extreme young Progressives in the world and as always with me it is my family right or wrong. Aint politics a funny thing to be so serious about? I take to such a man as Legge who could be friends with Hoover and Wilson both but loved farming better than men or methods. I believe in blackguarding like Hemmingway if you remember to burst out laughing when you get through. The only nonsense going is this talk about a revolution being on. Revolution with the Supreme Court still sitting undisturbed! You may have heard me say the greatest branch of any government the world ever saw is the Supreme Court of the United States. There it sits. A friend of mine named Landis has recently made a book called The Third American Revolution. I asked him where he got more than one. He thinks the victory of the North in the Civil War was a revolution that brought industry on top and overthrew agriculture. What licked the agriculture of the South was the agriculture of the Middle West under such Middle Westerners as Grant and Sherman. The industry that has swept the world was coming everywhere before the war and wasn't the least hastened by the war. One Revolution is all we have had and you'll wait more years than your allotted for a second. Don't let the Democrats worry you.

I wish I were where I could walk a block or two to

see you. Those streets from the Boulderado over just suited me. I suppose it was their contrast with the mountain roads, which even if I come out there to settle down, I shall always be afraid of."

There were changes in the house other than those brought on by the Democratic administration, but the events that sounded so dreadful to me never came off. "Going off the gold standard," as I heard it at the table, was to collapse the business structure of the world, and it was with great relief that the sun came up the next day and everything was quite as usual.

In the spring of 1933 Grandmother Bartlett died, but she'd been ill for some time following a broken hip, and her death seemed a natural event. We had seen her in 1928, and business prevented taking the trip East to her funeral. Aunt Ada inherited Grammy Bartlett's boarder and even "old John," whose death came not long after.

Forrest was losing interest in college engineering, disagreeing with his professors, who were fellow Rotarians, a source of embarrassment to John. Forrest had sinus trouble, too, and of course there was the girl he wanted to marry. I don't remember the reasons at the time, but he was sent out to California for several months and given a few trade journal assignments. Carol and Lillian, who were still in Monrovia, invited him to a picnic.

There was a tone of shocked despair about Forrest's failure at college, but Johnny's first year was worse. He out and out flunked. "Just not college material," my parents would say, shaking their heads and wondering what to do next.

The typewriters clicked on. The dictaphone still

"quack-quacked" as John turned out the manuscript for his third book, *Methods of Installment Selling and Collection*. Johnny was put to work distributing the *Daily Doings* in the summer, and there was a brief effort to interest Johnny in business by giving him the job of sending out letters to sell *Collection* stickers. It didn't prosper. I eventually used the sticker boxes for my paper dolls.

In the spring of 1934 Marjorie's baby was born; She was named Marjorie Robin, but was to be called Robin after her Grandfather Frost. It was happy news, the kind to send Margaret off into all the stories of the births of each of her babies. Her eyes would light up as she'd tell of her own joy of fulfillment, in spite of the drunken doctor when Johnny was born and her one experience with a hospital birth when Richard was born. She thought Richard's asthma was due to a difficult delivery in the hospital. When I was born, the doctor's son, just starting in practice, came to the farm, but lost his way trying to find our house in the country. "I had to hold you back until the doctor came, but as soon as the front door opened, I shouted, 'Shall I let her come?' And you slipped out so quickly I thought there must be another one! You should have seen Paul's big hands trying to dress you and putting the shirt on backwards!" She'd smile, remembering the scene, and then she'd feel anger again at the nurse who came to help, and frightened her by saying one of my legs was longer than the other. She fired the nurse. Over and over again she'd tell the stories, and I was so taken by the event of Robin's birth and intrigued by her name that I wrote a poem for a Camp Fire honor which began:

Robin was a little child
Born in spring when it was mild . . .

Elinor stayed with Marjorie for a few days after the birth, then returned home. Two weeks after Robin was born, a wire came from Willard informing Margaret and John that Marjorie was seriously ill with childbed fever. Without any hesitation John and Margaret turned their backs on the business and took the early train to Billings the next morning. No event had ever silenced the typewriters before.

They were in Billings when Rob and Elinor arrived from Amherst, Rob looking older than when they had last seen him in 1932, but better than they expected, as they had been told of his winter of extended colds and rheumatism. Rob appeared calm and more in command of himself than any of the family. John felt that Rob knew in full measure the gravity of Marjorie's illness, but kept hold of himself to strengthen Elinor and the others. "And there was something of the trouper's attitude of entertaining, regardless of the heartbreak beneath." John seems to have been a kind of straight man for the entertainer during those few days, helping to keep conversation going on general topics. Rob sought every opportunity to walk and talk with John, to let go of the worry, and discourse on other aspects of life.

Rob and Elinor's conference with the consulting doctor left them shaken, but they talked openly of the clinical diagnosis, puerperal fever. Elinor confided in Margaret, and Rob to John, that there was virtually no hope. Rob commented, "There are many stories in New England of mothers dying shortly after giving birth. It's written on the gravestones I've seen in cemeteries . . . probably the very same thing Marjorie is sick with."

Visiting Marjorie in the hospital, Rob said, "I plastered [the doctor] with pleasant remarks which I didn't feel. Elinor looked as if she disapproved, but I thought Marjorie would want me to, and I did it." Rob offered to relieve Willard who was near exhaustion, keeping watch in the hospital, but Marjorie said no; she wanted Willard. She called her mother and father into her room and insisted that under no circumstances was the line-up of doctors to be changed.

On walks with John, Rob discussed current reading: an article by James Norman Hall in the *Atlantic* discussing *Mutiny on the Bounty* and experiments in solitude. "There's something 'phony' about Thoreau's solitude, and I doubt that Hall could have a genuine experience in solitude. He'd be thinking in terms of the articles and books he was going to write. It isn't in man's nature to live an isolated life. Freedom isn't to be had that way. Going away and looking at man in perspective, and then coming back . . . an in and out existence . . . that is what's sane and good."

Frost told the story of going through the White Mountains and coming on an isolated farm, far back from the road. He'd walked over to ask for a glass of milk, and the farmer came to the door, mostly willin', but he'd continued to stand in the doorway, waving to cars as they passed on the road. "He's got that way since we came here," said the wife, "we're too far from people. He has to let people know he sees them."

In the field of poetry Frost talked about the erroneous theory that great experiences or great tragedies in personal lives produce great literary work. It's like the immorality among poets: "They think they are living intensely, as they say. They're only living loathesomely, and their verse is just flat, pages and pages neither good nor bad. As I used to say in the Academy days, just turn on the faucet. That's all you have to do to imagine Niagara Falls."

John, of course, was concerned with politics and how the country was going in the hands of Roosevelt. Rob generalized: "There's some socialism in every government . . . at least, every government based on mercy. The Socialists would have a government based wholly on mercy. It can't be done. Government based on justice, chiefly, with a measure of mercy, is the best we can hope to have."

"What is the democratic ideal?"

"One of moderation and restraint. Washington had an army behind him. So did Grant, and either could have taken the country, had anything. But they didn't. They stopped short of it. The supreme word isn't 'government,' it is civilization, the combination of many things: customs, ways of thinking, mores, religion, law, of course, but only a small part of the whole. . . . The great thing about America is the opportunity the individual has had to get up something himself. 'Let George do it.' George wants to do it, to have the chance to say, 'See what I've done.' We don't want to be regimented, directed, controlled."

John may have turned the conversation to talk about his own children, his worries about their seeming inability to handle college, although I never heard him discuss "personal worries" with anyone other than Margaret.

Rob knew a man who administered a top-rate school for eight hundred boys, but whose own sons had been in trouble with the police. "Sometimes I think, who is this who has failed with his own sons to be managing others?" But he concluded that the situation was not necessarily inconsistent. There could be men who were failures with their own sons, but good with the sons of others.

"My father hated his father; after he was fifteen he never took a cent from him . . . he drank and was wild. He was always going to take time off to cure his disease . . . consumption . . . but he never got around to it and died at thirty-five.

"He didn't care for me but he liked to have me with him downtown. He didn't care whether I went to school or not, and I never did. He was most concerned for my manners, for which he whipped me often. Mother would go into another room and pray.

"He licked me once with a chain. We had been out to a farm. There were pumpkins, and several times I had spoken my wish for one. My father had commanded silence. That night they came to the door; I answered and there was a jack-o'-lantern all lighted up, for me. I didn't accept it. I just said 'My father won't let me have it,' and slammed the door. I never saw a man more angry than he was then."

As for their own boys, Rob and John agreed: "Let them be what they want to be so long as it is honest. You can't put ambition into boys. It's up to them to take hold, catch on to life." Like a boy who is discouraged, Rob told the story of a horse hauling a tremendous load and, looking back, becoming frightened by it. A neighbor said, "He'll be worthless unless you cure him now."

"Can you cure him?"

"I'll show you," the owner said, and putting his hand on the horse's head calmed him and eased the fear. The horse pulled the load. "Give the discouraged boy something he can do, something that will give him the satisfaction of success."

Rob went on to speculate on the nature of his influence with his own family. "Do I exercise a soft tyranny? I've never had any trouble with any one of them. They speak out so seldom that it astonishes me when one does." Rob expressed disapproval of any principles or requirements of immediate success for children. "My best wish: that in success they wouldn't be too excited by it, or in failure too crushed. Young people should have a long life . . . and full of trouble. You can't have life without trouble."

"We all have our souls—and minds—to save, and it seems a miracle that we do it, not once, but many times. I can look back and see mine hanging by a thread. My sister wasn't able to save hers. She built the protecting illusion around herself and went the road of dementia praecox. Choice, somehow . . . will . . ."

There was no change in Marjorie's condition, just waiting. Margaret and John had to return to Boulder and business, having lent, for a brief time, the presence of old friends when there was nothing anyone could do.

Marjorie lingered with surprising strength, and in late April was taken by plane to the Mayo Clinic in Rochester, Minnesota, with the hope that skilled specialists could save her. She died there on May 2, 1934.

Her death was more than I, at eleven years of age,

could accept. My mother's efforts to comfort me—"She lived to have the greatest experience in a woman's life, to hold her own baby in her arms"—were shocking and unconvincing to me. It was not enough! What of Robin? And so I did not accept what I could not bear. Memories of Marjorie were permanently placed in the world of fairy tales, where princesses wear scarlet shawls at court balls and no one ever dies.

VII

1934-1940

DECIDING Johnny was "just not college material," John and Margaret felt they must give him some kind of trade training to prepare him for life. In the fall of 1934 Johnny was sent to Nashville, Tennessee, to a printing school. Forrest was sent to a radio school in Chicago, and the household, reduced in size, was more business-like than ever. John and Margaret did take a little time off—twice a week they would go to the movies; Sundays they would attend the Congregational church and we would go out for dinner afterward—eating at *Daily Doings* "trade-out" restaurants. Occasionally there would be an overnight stay in Denver at a hotel, a lobster dinner, and a show. Richard and I would go to the Sunday matinée,

first disapproved, but later conceded, because it allowed
John and Margaret to take a Sunday afternoon drive in
the hills up Sunshine Canon or the Gold Hill Road or
in the country to Haystack Mountain or Gunbarrel Hill.
The Sunday rides were Margaret's moments for poetry,
the brief wisps of time away from chattering typewriters,
manuscripts, and magazine dummies.

> You want to read?
> Then read, my dear,
> While I walk free, alone.
> A robin calls from leaf-thick tree,
> A chipmunk's making eyes at me.
> The pines are new in cone.
>
> Philosophy
> Of sage of old
> Inspires you, my dear?
> A nighthawk's flying in the blue,
> A magpie's teasing robins two,
> Their scoldings loud I hear;
>
> A penstemon,
> Dwarf specimen,
> Nods at me near my feet;
> A bit of sky on wings goes by,
> I hear the far off flicker's cry,
> Hushed murmuring of the creek.
>
> My soul expands,
> My spirit soars,
> Life's mysteries grow clear—
> How can you keep your eyes downcast
> On printed word of one long past,
> When God Himself's so near?

John kept up with Washington, reading the columnists, watching the political scene with the same intensity as that with which he now began to follow the Colorado Buffalo football team. He didn't attend the games, but he followed the broadcasts on Saturday. Every evening they'd drive down to put a batch of letters on the eleven o'clock train, then park the car on Lover's Hill to listen to the eleven o'clock newscast. A letter to Rob would undoubtedly have expressed concern for his country.

Frost, from his winter quarters in Florida, where he sought refuge from New England ice, had much to say on this same subject. His letter from Key West must have been written around January of 1935:

"I have been intending to write you a Christmas letter of consolation for the way things have been going with your adopted party and so by consequence with the republic. If only anything were clear it would be easier to talk. But there was a government once that began to put itself into the people, the object of its activity, to stiffen them so that there would be sure to be something there to govern. It kept doing for them out of the taxes till a day came when there [was] nothing positive enough left to tax. The last known it was making farmers pay taxes on any abandoned farm in their neighborhood as well as on their own. It was forcing the rich into the office of tax collector so that they could pay out of their own means what they failed to collect. The thing ran a while longer before it went to pieces and began all over. The pieces were a long time lying around loose. I can just see a little boy named Freddy Ordway looking at me in the class where we studied about that country. A

182

government must feel a funny lost feeling when it has nobody but its own reflection to govern. It must be grateful to gangsters (it shows itself grateful to gangsters you'll notice) for holding up their end in the conversation—the give and take between governor and governed. A cat can fool itself into thinking a spool has life of its own, but even a cat soon tires of the make-believe. What it wants is generations of mice coming on from sources it does not have to supply.

I paint a terrible picture of the past. The only fault I find with it is that like the pictures of winter in the north one reads in the Florida newspapers it may not be true. It may not be true of the past though history seems to say it is. It may have nothing in it to fear for the present. I don't see how we can get outside of things to know that without the danger of mental distension. All this may not be the decline of the west. I should feel sheepish to be too tragic about it. Let me not dramatize what, if it is happening, is too gradual over centuries for me to pretend honestly I can see it as drama. The most you and I can do is hang on to a few principles of religion and life by which to judge and act. Things may come out our way. Even those who seem against us may be for us. At any rate we shall have done our part.

One of the best things about the world is its badness. Is greed no more? Is competition over? Is war? It is our enemy who says so. It won't need us to confute them and all the thinking they are bound up in. To each fame according to his aspiration. No more in school or out of school shall we discriminate between first and second. I'm asked to suggest a plan for treating all authors alike. My answer is give everybody who claims to be an artist a minimum fame. A Cuban comes to my door with the worst painting I ever saw for sale. I say to him beamingly like a fond parent:

'You paint him?' (assuming that that's the way a Cuban would speak English.)

'Si Senor.'

'What for you no paint for Uncle Sam on the FERA?'

'Not bad enough to come in under.'

'You are not then, Senor, minimum-fame boy?'

He thinned his nose.

'All right I pay you minimum price.'

Down by the aquarium has Franklin D set up a studio for northern artists on the rocks. It makes me mad this young Cuban pretender isn't taken into it. But I have been madder before and done nothing about it. And sadder too.

Affectionately

R.

I failed to get this poem to you sooner for want of proper governmental incentive. It's not that I don't know where I am these days. I'm as tough and self-possessed as ever. But where I am has been too many places. For a month I was on the road with my annual allowance of lectures and then home hunting for us two and on top of that for Carol, Lillian, and Prescott. We found it harder this time to get satisfied. This town is an interestingly shabby place with a history of by gone piracy smuggling and finally Cuban cigar manufacturing over here from Cuba to get inside the tarriff wall. All is gone except the hope of becoming a popular Florida resort. That hope has dwindled since its height twenty years ago when the railroad came in over sea bridges from small key to key.

Streets were laid out then with concrete walks and es-
planades along the beaches. A few houses got started but
only a few. The fifty thousand expected haven't come
yet. The native population has shrunk from 25,000 to
12,000. I don't believe the natives know what they are
missing. Their only trouble has been hunger. They have
eaten the wild life out of existence since 1929 and they
gobble up the coconuts as fast as they fall. The town is
spotted with good old houses of former prosperity. Close
around these are hovels and hovels. You may have read
this is one of the Government's chief projects. Some idea
was entertained of moving a lot of the wretchedest away
but nobody wanted to go and nobody knew where to
put them. So a whole trainload of the FERA descended
on the town to save it by reviving the real estate boom
with propaganda and public works. The FERA has
taken over the renting of all houses and the cleaning up
of ruins and rubbishful lots. It has reopened the swell
beach hotel (with a big noise last night which was New
Years). We don't know what we think of it and don't
need to know. Carol and Lillian arrived yesterday having
done 17000 miles from South Shaftsbury. It's an accident
and an adventure (just one more). We had no idea of
finding anything like the FERA here and bulking so
large in proportion. The weather beats all—day and night
temperatures the year round between 60 and eighty.
Very little difference between summer and winter.
Water all off the roof from autumn rains. No rain in
winter. Air might be too soft for some. Somewhat humid
as you might expect on a South Sea island. Soil rather
thin on the coral. Stores small town and poorish. I
couldn't find a manilla envelope high or low. Library

nothing. Naval station, army post customs house. Cuban orchestra."

Family affairs gave relief of sorts from disgust at the way the country was going. Johnny found printing and Tennessee and living in a boarding house not to his liking, and, besides, he'd left behind in Boulder a girl he'd decided he was seriously interested in marrying. He hocked his grandfather's watch for bus fare home, talked University officials into enrolling him again, and then presented himself on our doorstep. When he graduated from the business school at the University with an A average, John, Sr., beamed with pride: "That's the Bartlett in him!"

It was a remark we often heard when we did something that pleased him. Richard, the frail one of the family with an inclination to asthma, had been so wrought up by having to play an accordion solo in front of the junior high school that he lost a night's sleep. He gave up accordion playing, but went on to debating and public speaking. "That's the Bartlett spirit."

Forrest, completing his radio course, married his high-school sweetheart, and in the midst of the depression found a job at KFEL radio station in Denver at fifteen dollars a week. "The Bartlett determination," John would say. Margaret sometimes expressed annoyance that if the children did anything right, it was credited to Bartlett. She may have been saving "That's the Abbott!" for valedictorians. None of us were.

In the summer of 1935 we bought a house on Mapleton Hill in a "good section" of town. "The house that words built," Margaret called it. Times may have been terrible, but we moved ahead, even out of the Essex class to a second-hand Plymouth sedan. The gears were so silent in comparison to our old car that John once drove from Denver to Boulder in second gear. Shifting was no better though. We just braced for the lurch. Usually, John took the bus to Denver, staying only the day and returning with a bundle of *Author and Journalist* mail, a bag of pinion nuts, and "Say, I heard a good story today. The fellow I sat with on the bus had been a cattle rancher, and he . . ."

We were barely settled in our Pine Street house when Rob and Elinor came for the Writer's Conference again. It was the first time since Marjorie's death that John had seen them, and Willard came down from Billings with Robin, his mother, and brother Jack. Robin had spent some time in the East with Carol and Lillian, but the tearing of the emotions, shifting her back and forth, was too much for the family to bear. Rob decided it was better to have her brought up in Montana with Willard and her grandmother. The Frasers stayed with us, Rob and Elinor at the Boulderado Hotel.

I remember sitting on the bench under our apple tree talking to Elinor. Her voice was quiet, her eyes tearful, but without tears. In her hands she clutched a ball of a handkerchief and an abused pack of cigarettes. She seemed cool, distant, and her smile was only a remote suggestion, as if she meant "some other time, not now."

But Rob, John noted as soon as he greeted the Frosts at the station in Denver, looked fresh, vigorous, and happy, "never more so." On earlier visits he had frequently mentioned at the outset people he wanted to avoid meeting. This time he immediately asked about

187

the Writer's Conference: "How's it going?" John explained that Rob was coming in the middle of a hot and disrupting controversy. Edward Davison, the Program Director, believed in "art for art's sake," and had announced that "a writer who wrote for money is both a fool and a rascal." On the other side stood the Conference Director, Walter M. Campbell, and Mrs. Blanche McNeal, short-story writer and member of the University Extension staff, who stressed not only how to write but how to sell. Each side had gathered friends and supporters, and hostilities were rising close to the surface.

Rob immediately told John his coming to the Conference was through a "deal" with Ted Davison, made in Florida during the winter. He'd wanted to do something for his daughter Lesley, who'd been teaching during the past year in Illinois, and had agreed to come to the Writer's Conference in Boulder in exchange for Lesley's being offered a summer position teaching contemporary poetry at the University of Colorado. "I'll make a trade," he told John. "I often do . . . But I don't care much about doing it, or the people I trade with. Still, I'm enough of a Yankee to view a trade a trade and handle my side of it with skill."

As it turned out, Lesley wired she was unable to fulfill the engagement. Ted Davison, an Englishman with a red bulbous nose and fiery eyes, was furious. "I've been mistreated!" he told John, but Frost was not to be drawn into a discussion—at the Davison home he spent his time entertaining the young Davison children with a ten-cent Mickey Mouse book.

Mid-week in the Conference it became apparent that the program was likely to suffer if the gathering hostile forces came to a showdown. Frost had steered clear of such controversies in earlier years. This time he carried his weight, talking with the head of the University summer school and deciding to talk to George Norlin, the President of the University. Rob liked Dr. Norlin, "a sweet, open man," but had been miffed at not hearing from him after his arrival in Boulder. In this case he set his personal feelings aside to seek the President out at the faculty ranch. "I told him I hadn't intended to visit him," Rob related to John. "And he replied that since I ignored his letters and telegrams he decided he wasn't under any obligation to see me." Each understanding the other's attitude, they amiably discussed the row that threatened to disrupt the Conference.

Returning to Boulder, Frost talked to each side in such a mannerly way that both sides seemed to feel he supported their views. He confided in John, however, that he felt the Campbell-McNeal side had the sounder view, representing all things, but as for holding a position of "Shakespeare to the pulps," he could only be *for* Shakespeare in such a situation.

The climax of the controversy was the Conference dinner, with speakers charging certain men with "plotting in their cups" to get rid of other members of the staff. It was awkward and embarrassing, and Ted Davison, as master of ceremonies, apologized that "such matters were below the dignity of Mr. Frost, who incidentally agrees with me." Frost fidgeted at being misrepresented, but remained silent while Whit Burnett, of *Story* magazine, gave the main talk of the evening. When he made the statement that "all good stories are the product of either sex or drink," Rob penciled a note to Davison requesting that he not be called on to speak. As he told John later, driving home, "I hardly felt adequate to such an occasion. My stories don't come from either sex or drink." He didn't speak at the dinner.

Rob talked with John about the question of writing for money. It was a "silly" dispute, he said. One of Wordsworth's chief interests after he was forty was money, and certainly he was a great poet. He mentioned being invited to lecture at a writers' conference in Greeley and being offered a cut-rate price of $150 (usual fee, $200) because he was already so close by in Boulder. He turned it down. "Being a poet isn't like an amateur tennis player who is regarded as somewhat sinful if he 'goes professional' and takes pay. To establish himself, a poet has to separate himself from the amateurs, and the pay he receives is a kind of index of his worth." Sometimes he'd lecture for nothing, when he felt like it and it might help someone, but he had more requests for lectures than he could grant. He seemed to enjoy turning down some, especially if he felt somebody was trying to "get me cheap."

During this visit, he went down to Santa Fe to lecture, mostly out of friendship for Witter Bynner. Rob liked some of his verse, and Bynner had befriended him in earlier years. Before leaving on the train by himself, Rob asked John if he could borrow his copy of *Collected Poems* because he hadn't brought along a copy of his own. "Probably somebody down there would have a copy," but he did not wish to embarrass anyone by making a request and forcing people to reveal they didn't own a Frost book.

"I shouldn't have gone down there," he remarked when

he returned. It seems that Bynner was enthusiastic about a vanity-published book that Rob thought "one of the vilest things I ever read." Frost could go so far as to say "the work is striking," but could concede no more. He felt grateful for other friends who helped him avoid meetings with Bynner where the controversy would be resumed.

The big event of the summer, in fact, the largest entertainment ever arranged by Margaret, was a Conference Tea in our new house. Two hundred people were invited, but Rob, having been up late the night before and eaten food that was too rich, only stood up through part of it. Elinor, for all she looked worn and unwell, stayed the afternoon, greeting all comers. The greatest wonder to me, who was appointed to direct people to the punch bowl and the exit through the den (office) door, was the marvelously horrifying sight of Thomas Wolfe, who was on the Conference staff that summer. The towering blackheaded giant with piercing eyes held his cup of orange sherbet in ginger ale like a doll's teacup in his oversized hand, and took his position leaning against the magazine desk in the den. *I* knew that the leg on the desk had been broken in moving, and that it was just propped in place. I think I showed fifty people out the door before he moved, but the leg held. I don't know if it was ever fixed.

John and Margaret both found time to attend Rob's lectures, although they never attended many Conference lectures otherwise. "How did this lecture compare with my early ones, like the one in Exeter in the winter of 1916?" he asked John.

John answered that his apparent ease was infinitely

greater, and the immediate rapport he managed to establish with the audience formed a marked contrast to the earlier lecture.

Some lectures, Rob confessed, still had him in a state of confusion, and he couldn't eat. Others he enjoyed. But he wondered: "The audience liked 'To a Thinker in Office' [published the next year under the title "To a Thinker"]. Did they think I was talking about Roosevelt?" The poem was written in 1934 before many of the things included in it had come true. "I jested with them [the audience]. Maybe they don't take me seriously enough. Maybe that kind of a lecture is dangerous."

He had answered, in his first lecture of the Conference, the accusation that he was an escapist, running away to the country and seeking solitude. "What one person calls an escapist might really be a pursuitist, like the man who climbed the apple tree not to get away from the ground and the world but to reach the apples."

Time was too limited, and there were too many relatives around, to enjoy leisurely talk with Rob during this visit, but John commented to Margaret that he looked better and stronger than any time in the almost thirty years they'd known him: more tranquil, less affected by concerns and irritations. He acted the master of situations.

They hoped to see him on a quick trip East to the twenty-fifth reunion of their Pinkerton class, but had to be content with his wire instead:

JOHN AND MARGARET. WHY WOULD YOU GO HAVING PARTIES AT A TIME OF YEAR WHEN I CAN'T COME TO THEM? IF YOU DON'T CALL ON US ON YOUR WAY HOME

It was too hasty a trip to make the detour to see Rob,
and they didn't see him again for four years.

In the meantime, national affairs moved along to another election crisis. John had great faith in the *Literary
Digest* poll, which showed that Alf Landon had the
strength to knock Roosevelt out of office in 1936. John
wore a necktie with a yellow sunflower and passed out
campaign buttons for his children and his friends to wear.
The day after election was even worse than when we
went off the gold standard. John came to the table with
heavy steps. He pushed the silverware aside; how could
anyone eat? He put his elbow on the table and rested
his head in his hand. Surely this was the end, a country
doomed to Democratic control for another four years.

John turned from his despair to serious political work,
devoting more time to the Republican cause. He lobbied
for the Hardware Association against the sales tax before
the Denver legislature. Such activities brought in no
money, but Margaret was handling Boulder *Daily Doings*
and much of *The Author and Journalist*, catching up
John's fresh ideas as he'd toss them her way. "Introducing
a new post on our staff is that of Poll Director, and
Molly Adams is the first to fill it," *The Author and
Journalist* notice read. Molly Adams was Margaret, under
whose name questionnaires were sent out and the replies
sifted for editorial use or an article.

By 1938 John was thoroughly involved in politics. He
managed the campaign for William S. Hill for Congress,
lost that year; but Colorado gained a Republican gov-

ernor. Things were looking up. In November, when elections were broadcast—in the year the University of Colorado had a winning football team with Whizzer White the star player, John sitting by the radio in the living room with a clipboard on his knee, following each play and gain of yards—he also charted the election returns as they came in for each candidate, with a slap on the knee and a cheer for every Republican win.

The news of Elinor's death in Florida in 1938 reached them through a newspaper account. Rob did not write many letters, and it was by accident, at the World Press in Denver where *The Author and Journalist* was published, that John happened to notice tickets being printed for a Frost lecture in the winter of 1939. They had heard bits of information: that Robert Frost was to be present at the dedication ceremonies of the new Poetry Room at the University of Wyoming and had been invited to take part in the Honors Convocation at the University of Colorado, but he had not answered their letters inviting him to stay with the family. Doing a little detective work, they ferreted out his schedule, and sent a wire to Edmond, Olahoma, asking to be allowed to meet him. A wire came Sunday night: "Hope you can meet me in Denver Monday 8:15 A.M."

Meeting Rob coming up out of the train subway, John and Margaret were startled to see him looking "unexpectedly well," in spite of the fact he told them he had been suffering from intestinal flu for the past two days. He looked older than in 1935, but his conversation in the car was sure and clear. He had to stay with the Norlins, he said, to please them, but asked to be driven to the Bartlett home for a little talk first.

Elinor's death was on everyone's mind, and Rob immediately plunged into talk of Elinor. They had been difficult years, these past ones. Elinor had lost her old firmness; burdened herself with worry over the children, unable to let go. The children swayed her, and her bitter resentment over the New Deal and Roosevelt kept her awake nights, consuming her strength in worrying over the fate of the country.

Rob's address that afternoon at the Honors Convocation, where he was awarded an honorary degree, was not good form, for him. "I was pulling a load all the way," he told John, although his audience was with him and was disappointed when he stopped, quite abruptly, after a half-hour. He talked of educational theories and emphasis, weaving in some of the talk he'd had with John and Margaret on the drive from Denver that morning. John had remarked that my high school was taken up with "progressive education," and that "they don't ask what you learn, but how many committees are you on."

"Restraint, Force, and Material," Frost told his audience, "with the greater emphasis on Material. It isn't education unless you approached it with ABC's or 1-2-3's." He mentioned the Poetry Room which he was to dedicate in Laramie, constructed and decorated to "seduce students to read." "It reminds me of the story in Lawrence of the saloon-keepers putting beer in the sprinklers and sprinkling the sawdust outside the entrance to seduce the youth of the city. A university should be a manufacturer of self-starters."

At the Honors dinner that night: "I didn't expect to have strength for it, but Plato saved me." He was "set off" by the remarks of a classics professor who quoted

Plato and spoke of scholars becoming rascally or useless. "Professor Dyde should have gone on to speak of the unscrupulousness of the executive mind. The executive mind runs government, university departments, and athletic teams, and it never sticks at trifle. 'I don't want wisdom,' it says; 'I want accomplishment.' A high government official said to me, talking about the TVA, 'All we do is take away from some the right to be a bad farmer.' And that is just what is wrong with it!" The audience immediately warmed to his talk, and even Dr. Norlin, ordinarily a sad, bored-looking man at public gatherings, sat with a rapt smile of attention, breaking into laughter at some of Frost's allusions.

"There was a lady who had one operation and was going to have another. She complained to me that it left her unable to do anything. 'Why not think?' I told her. 'Will you put that down on paper for me?'"

John had never seen Rob perform so brilliantly, inspired from beginning to end.

After the first night at Dr. Norlin's, Rob used the Bartlett home as base, going to Fort Collins, Denver, and Colorado Springs for lectures. With the exception of the Colorado Springs lecture, which was part of a Fine Arts Conference, he was pleased with his audiences and the lectures went well. The trouble with the Colorado Springs lecture: "Not my kind of affair. I like a one-man show."

Richard, now a freshman in college, had driven Rob back from the Springs. Rob had purposely left behind his dress clothes to avoid a dinner the night before, and had gone to see *Pygmalion* instead. His only luggage was a small, damaged overnight case with the snap broken. He'd borrowed a strap to hold it together.

Between lectures he'd sit in the living room and tell stories to John about his farm-buying ventures and experiences dealing with "my old enemies." Some talk was playful, in seeming fun, but he'd sum it up: "It was really an ugly incident."

John had pointed out the Stearns Dairy sign outside of Denver. It was at the dairy that Johnny had managed to find employment in the business office when jobs were hard to come by. He was married now, and John told of Forrest in California, working for Transradio Press, with his wife expecting a baby—all going well, although there had been ups and downs working at radio stations during the hard times of the thirties.

Rob talked about his concern for his son, Carol. "He seems to lack 'grasp' . . . taking hold of one end of a thing and forgetting the other." He'd talked it over with Lesley; maybe the best thing to do was for Rob to leave enough, and so fixed, that Carol would always be sure to have ample. "But it sounds too much like giving up hope for Carol, and I don't like that."

As he left to continue his lecture tour, both John and Margaret wondered at Rob's new restlessness and eagerness to be on the move, his energy and vigor that moved outward. "Are the new circumstances of being 'on his own,' unaccompanied by Elinor, the cause of it?" John asked Margaret.

"It accounts for his being less neat than usual," she answered.

VIII

The Forties

FROST left Amherst after Elinor's death, and in the forties spent summers at the Homer Noble Farm in Ripton, Vermont, winters in Florida, and "in-between" seasons at his Cambridge, Massachusetts, house. His teaching and lecturing did not bring him to Colorado again.

John managed to put his candidate, William S. Hill, into Congress in 1940, which helped ease the third successive Republican defeat in the White House. Richard and I were off to college, but the house had its staff of office workers, busier than before because *The Author and Journalist*, which John had owned with Willard Hawkins of Denver, was now a John T. and Margaret A. Bartlett publication. The basement of the house was remodeled into an office, with two regular "mailing girls," while the secretary kept the typewriter in the office going, transcribing the cylinders dictated by both John and Margaret.

Margaret would work at the typewriter after supper at night, to keep the Bartlett Syndicate Service going. Full ownership of *The Author and Journalist* brought extra tasks, not only the many personal notes Margaret would write to subscribers, but the Criticism Service, too. For years they'd kept the rigid rule of not working Sundays, but now there were deadlines, proofs to be read, and the pile of manuscripts to go through that couldn't be fitted into any other day. Handling the Criticism Service, Margaret would go through each submission, painfully aware of the hopes and aspirations of the writer, and try to give honest, helpful suggestions to some unbelievably bad material. She couldn't bear to lose a subscriber over a "kick," and if someone wrote: "Cancel my subscription! The idea of a magazine of your standards using a cover picture showing an author smoking a cigarette!"—Margaret would patiently soothe the ruffled spirits, and more often than not keep the subscriber.

Both of them developed a highly personal feeling toward their *Author and Journalist* audience; they gave help to writers in every medium: pulps, slicks, nonfiction, poetry. They emphasized sales, and each issue contained a success story. They investigated rackets, exposed fraudulent contests, and John, of course, kept his readers informed of legislation to protect the writers' interests (usually sponsored by Republicans). They increased their *Author and Journalist* "family" from 10,000 to 17,000 subscribers, and started a "Mostly Personal" column for comments, to talk over ideas, and tell about their children.

Margaret could barely discuss Roosevelt or foreign affairs, fearing "that war-monger" would take sons from their mothers to use as fodder in his private war interests. (The country did become involved in a war, but her own boys were all disqualified from the draft for one or another physical reason.) Such feelings of anger as she'd passionately display at the table, she would, on her Sunday afternoon rides, turn into a positive thought: a poem. She won the First Award in the Poetry Contest of the National Federation of Press Women in 1943 with "Victory Harvest."

> There are golden tents on the plains today,
> Bristling with golden spears;
> There are millions of soldiers hid within—
> Yet never a sound one hears
>
> Save the crackly rustle like silken skirt
> As the wind blows softly through
> Those tents that are guarding a nation's life
> Guarding your home—and you;
>
> For the soldiers hidden beneath those tents
> Are golden grains of wheat
> Who can turn the tide of battles
> And wrest Victory from Defeat!

News from Rob, in the forties, was only what was read in the papers. The news that Carol had ended his life by committing suicide somehow didn't surprise them, but they wondered about Lillian, his wife, and Prescott, growing to young manhood. No letters were received from Rob until concern about family illness brought a call to his old friends. He wrote from Cambridge, Massachusetts, on January 20, 1943:

"This is just to tell you and Margaret there's another Frost in trouble in your region. I hope the trouble isn't going to prove very serious. Prescott, just past eighteen, enlisted a month or so ago in the Signal Corps and was sent to Camp Carson for his basic training. All well and good so far. But now comes word that he has gone down with pneumonia and partly recovered—all in one message. Probably he has been given some of the new medicine I won't attempt to spell. There is nothing you can do. But I thought if he was invalided out temporarily and not sent clear home he might find time on his hands and you might help him spend it by asking him for a night's visit at Boulder. I reminded him in my only letter so far that he had you or the thought of you for moral support not too far off. I don't know what such a sickness means to the army doctors and how it will affect Prescott's career as a soldier. I wait for further news with some anxiety. The further news has just this minute come in through the slot in the front door. The pneumonia was the bad kind and he was probably only saved by the drug I can't spell the name of. That changes nothing I have said above. Prescott may write to you some time along. He may sign his name Prescott as of old, but it is to be noticed that the army has decided to know him as Private William P. Frost. His great grandfather, my father, was always called William Frost though he had the same Prescott for a middle name.

I wish I could see you. There is some chance of my going by and dropping in on my way to engagements in California next fall if the war doesn't cancel them. I thought I would be out entirely but I am still hired now and then by people who can bear to hear something talked about besides the war. I can talk about the war upon occasion, but what unfits me for most platforms is that most people believe in this war only whereas I believe in any and all wars. I mean I sympathize with all the brave people who go out to die for causes. They are the great boys, beside whom I am nothing."

Prescott spent a weekend with the Bartletts, charming everybody with his easy manner of talking, and a gift for story-telling and humor "like his grandfather." Both John and Margaret expressed relief: "He's kept his hands off Prescott! Not too much interference!"

By 1944 I was out of college and in the Navy, patriotic but safe. The closeness of the war was felt in 1945 when Forrest went to the Philippines with a civilian press wireless group, setting up a mobile unit to transmit news to the United States in MacArthur's wake. John reported proudly to his *Author and Journalist* readers: "The first two weeks on Leyte brought such novel and challenging experiences as to maintain the station without tools— they hadn't arrived yet from the States, and substitute gadgets had to be devised; repairing delicate high speed communications apparatus with the aid of a flashlight, standing in water and amid the crashing din of ack-ack fire; three days of dengue fever (Forrest remained on the job). During this period the PW men got acquainted with slit trenches, saw their first zeros shot down."

All the children were now "on their own"; two grandsons assuring that the Bartlett name would be carried on. They were out from under the financial burden of their children, "ambition sparkers," as Margaret wrote in one of her *Author and Journalist* articles. In spite of the economic restrictions, the difficulties of getting paper during the war, their small publications did very well. They talked of "letting up" and "easing off." John's health seemed to be giving way, with more severe attacks of asthma, and his color wasn't good; there was a gray, unhealthy look about him. When they made a train trip East to the Mayo's in the spring of 1945, they had to wire ahead to a station stop and have a doctor come aboard to give John an adrenalin shot to relieve an acute asthmatic attack. Somehow, sickness gave them the inclination to remember old friends, and they sent a post card from Rochester to Rob, in part to request a copy of his newly published *A Masque of Reason.*

Frost answered from Ripton, Vermont, on June 15, 1945:

"It's a case of the climate's having worn out I suppose. The last election can't have done it to you, you got so much compensation for the general badness in having carried Colorado. And whether we like the philosophy or not we can't refuse the comfort of knowing that any time we please we can loaf six months of a year at twenty-five dollars a week. Twenty five a week is more than I ever earned till I was forty. We old-time shoe-string starters mustn't ask everybody to be like us.

The picture of the sky scraper full of doctors and nurses in the prairie gave me no special delight. It's a great place out there in the middle. It's good to have such a resort in time of sickness and death. I don't know how much I owe it though. Not much, I'd say. There was one doctor among them all I remember with respect for his honest good sense. I hope you and Margaret found someone to solve your problems. Almost anyone, you'd think, might write you out a diet.

Forrest must have been right up into the thing. My heart is with those only who made the real sacrifice. I've hardly been touched. Prescott's health has been impared by his pneumonia three times and he was genuinely disappointed in being rejected as a soldier. He talked of intending a military career. Lesley is in Madrid in charge of the American Library and our cultural relations with the Spanish. That is I hope she is. She flew away to Europe two or three weeks ago. The only letter from her is dated from our Embassy at Lisbon and speaks as if she had jumped from the hot water of the OWI in New York into boiling oil there. I don't dare to guess what she means by boiling oil. There is barbarous conflict in her own department and then of course there is the more or less latent political revolution in the country. The Russians are there in disguise and so are the British. I don't know what we poor innocents think we are doing between them.

I saw Margaret Jr. at Northampton looking fine in her uniform of a WAC [WAVE] officer.

You must have a Masque from me of course.
                    As of old at Pinkerton
                    and on Patuckaway

                                        Rob"

The trip was unsatisfactory and inconclusive, and resulted in no change of habits. There was talk of taking a trip to Medicine Hat where they were married, and

Margaret saved out Canadian coins and currency sent in by Canadian subscribers to use on their sentimental journey. But monthly, weekly, and quarterly deadlines left little time for travel. Margaret anxiously watched John using his strength to handle the publicity for a local bond issue (successful), and his work as Republican Chairman for the Second Congressional District. The danger signs of deteriorating health were there, yet it somehow seemed safer to "keep things going" than make any change, as if making a concession to ill health would admit a fear they did not want to recognize. John eased up enough to do more reading after dinner in the evening, but Margaret returned to the office. She had a fondness for Bartlett Syndicate Service and hated to let it go.

In January, 1947, John was stricken with a severe abdominal pain and rushed to the hospital, where he died five days later of a coronary thrombosis.

All the children came home to be at his bedside, taking turns being with him during the day, while Margaret tended business at home; at night she slept on a cot in his room. Returning to the house after he died, Margaret set to work to get *The Author and Journalist* copy ready. She told her readers in the "Mostly Personal" column: "It is with a torn and lonely heart that I must tell you that John will be with you no more . . . It is going to be hard going on without John, for our work and our play, our hopes and our dreams, all were merged. Married since 1912, we had had a wonderful life together. This issue was produced under great difficulties. Only one article had been prepared when John was taken ill. Getting the rest of the book together while every night I stayed close by John at the hospital, carrying two loads daytime, was almost more than could be accomplished. The result is far from perfect, but I know you will understand that I did my best under the circumstances."

With no shedding of tears, she handled the business, and, as she explained to her *Author and Journalist* readers, when the emptiness of the house oppressed her after the office staff left, she bought a cat for companionship and took to reading biographies, while she ate supper, to combat loneliness. The mechanics of her life held her to a straight course.

The first summer after John's death she received a letter from Earl Anderson, a newspaperman in New Hampshire whom John had encouraged early in his career, offering his services. She wrote back, "However extensive our interests were, they were still so much of a personal nature that there never seemed room for anyone else. Even now that I am alone, there seems no way to take anyone, unless it would be one of the children, into partnership, or even as a paid assistant. The work is probably too much for one person, but it is not enough for two, unless the two were one as John and I were. . . ."

She wrote with satisfaction that *Daily Doings* had more advertising than ever before, that *The Author and Journalist* had picked up 750 subscribers, and that, with help on the legislative problems, she was handling the Hardware Association secretaryship until its conclusion the following year.

"Just how long I shall continue to carry such a burden I don't know. John would never be satisfied for me to go on doing so much detail, and tieing myself so securely to a desk. He had always said that he knew that he was going to go before I did and that he hoped that I would have an opportunity to get out from under the heavy load I have carried for so many years, and devote myself to personal writing. That is in the back of my mind. . . .

"Of course health will be a determining factor, too. I am quite well, but not 100% by any means. . . . I feel I have what Mother Bartlett used to call 'vital tenacity,' and expect that, despite many things I know are not quite right, I shall be active for many years. Not that I hope for a long life. It is so terribly hard to face long years ahead without the companionship of John. I am quite skillful at 'putting on a show' before folks, so that everybody feels that I have adjusted wonderfully, taken John's passing in a surprisingly easy way, but they don't know the pain and emptiness underneath the 'false front' that doesn't go away, doesn't ease up. Everybody thinks I have so much to be thankful for (I have) and so much that I should be happy for (and I have) and yet, I would gladly and instantly give up everything just to be with John."

The health that was "not quite right" turned out to be cancer, but she kept silent for several months, knowing "something was wrong" before seeing her doctor. Within a week after the diagnosis of cancer was made, she underwent surgery, but with no interruption in the monthly publication of *The Author and Journalist*. She told her readers: "Yes, I'm still here! I told you I had 'bounce'— and I proved it! Despite blood transfusions, the drip-drip-drip of glucose solution into my veins, the frequent jabs of the hypodermic needle with penicillin and morphine, breathing under the oxygen tent for hours on end, long picture-painted sleep induced by drugs—on the sixth day

I walked, on the tenth day I was allowed to go home, on the 13th day I went up and down stairs, and a few days later I discarded robe and slippers, dressed down to my very own shoes, had the dictaphone moved into my room, and told myself it was time to go to work!"

The Boulder *Daily Doings* appeared regularly and on time; the *Mt. Hardware Dealer* was fat with postwar advertising; and *The Author and Journalist* readers received their helps and a monthly recounting of family affairs: two new grandsons ("still hoping for a granddaughter"); Johnny had passed his CPA examinations; Richard was teaching American history at Texas A. & M.; Forrest's radio articles appeared in *CQ* and *QST*. Writing "on her own," except for a poem now and then which she'd use in the *Daily Doings*, was impossible. Time and energy were used up carrying on the routine of years.

The letters from Robert Frost, stuffed in a manila envelope in the back of the bottom drawer of the Winthrop desk, weighed on her mind. With physical strength slipping downhill, Margaret began to think in terms of "finishing up." The story of the friendship with Frost, and the letters which had been saved, though unsorted and unread for many years, was unfinished business, and she wrote asking Rob's permission to publish the letters with the story. He answered from Cambridge on December 26, 1947:

"You would have several advantages over anyone else that might attempt my biography. I mean anyone else outside of my own family. Only Lesley's memories would go back further and go in deeper than yours. That ought to make me afraid of you. But its not from fear that I must ask you to spare me another ordeal of the kind in my lifetime. It is from something I find it hard to explain or even talk about. I am sick at heart from having had my picture taken and my portrait painted. Having my life written up is as bad. I am having it right now by one and threatened by several others. Much more and I will stop being an active man and sit back in a pose merely self-conscious. Let me tell you what I wish you would do: write anything you please about me, but put off publishing it till I am dead and gone. You ought to be able to outlive me. If you find you aren't, you can pass the documents you create on to your most trustworthy heir. Then for both of us the glory will be posthumous. This is permission for you to tell anything you please on me, but to posterity. Now let's pretend you haven't spoken to me in the matter and I will try not to think about what you may be busy with. Do I seem to make too much of myself in all this talk of avoiding self-consciousness? I know it is not important whether my life is written up or not. All the same if you want to please me you will take it off my mind that I may have to face another version of my fortunes and misfortunes. The latter pile up as the years run. You may not have heard the sad ending to Irma's story. She is at once too insane to be out of an institution and too sane to be in one. So she suffers the sense of imprisonment where she is, in one. But I didn't start this letter to let you further into my dismalities. I have things to be thankful for. I have friends for instance. I have had you and John."

The letters remained in the envelope. Deadlines seemed to come up with greater frequency, demanding immediate attention; time was racing by with proofs to correct, advertising to okay, subscription circulars to get out. Through part of this time I was home to help out, and sometimes Margaret talked to me of her dream that I would stay home and together we would manage *The Author and Journalist*, but she didn't hold me back when I returned to California to follow my own interests. To stay her emptiness of spirit, after the business of the day, she'd write "letters to John" in a notebook before going to sleep at night, holding fast, as she'd tell me, to the memories of her life with John, "like jewels in a bag of gems."

A gnawing pain in her back eroded the strength that she had seemed to gain immediately after her operation. She had no doubt that it was a recurrence of cancer, but a trip to Mayo's did not establish the fact. In the fall of 1949, having let go of only the Hardware Association business, she underwent an operation (severing the nerve in her lower back) to relieve her pain. Completely bed-ridden and fed intravenously, she conducted her business from the Pine Street bedroom, with a dictaphone in her hand most of her waking hours. She had completed the summer of *Daily Doings* and was determined to "complete the 1949 *Author and Journalist* book" before turning the magazine over to new owners. She felt, as she told her readers, a personal commitment to see that the magazine was sold to the "right" publisher who would be as personally concerned with reader's problems as she and John had been.

Alan Swallow of Denver had seen her poetry and offered to publish a volume of her verse, collected from many publications throughout the years. The collection, entitled *Afterglow*, was to be her Christmas greeting and final message to her friends.

In a notebook, in handwriting that remained firm and unchanged in spite of her illness, she began chapter one of the Frost story. But it was only John she could see, recounting her "coolness" when she'd thought she was too young to be in love, and Frost's saying, "Go talk to John, Margaret. He's miserable." She wrote of Frost's touching her arm when he "jumped the gun" on the faculty decision, telling her with pride that she was valedictorian; how he'd winked at John, third honors, and said "Love and studies don't mix." Rob had understood. Although she'd many times told me the story of Frost's coming to Pinkerton on the strength of "A Tuft of Flowers," now she substituted a different poem, "The Flower Boat."

> The fisherman's swapping a yarn for a yarn
> Under the hand of the village barber,
> And here in the angle of house and barn
> His deep-sea dory has found a harbor.
>
> At anchor she rides the sunny sod
> As full to the gunnel of flowers growing
> As ever she turned her home with cod
> From George's bank when winds were blowing.
>
> And I judge from that Elysian freight
> That all they ask is rougher weather,
> And dory and master will sail by fate
> To seek for the Happy Isles together.

In October she told her *Author and Journalist* readers that she had written Rob again requesting permission to publish the letters, one final task she hoped to complete before her death. She thanked her readers for cards and letters sent in response to the announcement of her terminal illness in the previous issue. "How I wish I could send a personal note to each writer! But I know not one of you expects that, as strength has hardly been sufficient to cover the work on this November issue. My heart is warm with love for you. I am full of fight should it be God's will for me to get well, but full of content and eagerness if He is beckoning 'Come.'"

Early in November Margaret was taken to the hospital, but she managed to read the December *Author and Journalist* proofs, to "finish the book." She wrote, in still recognizable script, personal inscriptions on the flyleaves of her book of poems, pages fresh from the printers, still unbound. Rob's letter came on November 24th, but Margaret had slipped into a coma: a childlike sleeping face, a body almost without weight on the white hospital bed. But his answer of November 22, 1949, held true the tone of all the years, looking behind the impulse of the moment and the immediate fears to the strength beneath:

"All the more in an emergency like this I seem disinclined to let you make a publisher's venture of the letters I wrote you and John in the simplicity of the heart back there when none of us was anybody . . .

I take it your main idea is to put the record of our friendship beyond danger of being lost. Let me suggest one way you could do that without sacrilege. You could deposit the letters as a lot with one of the three or four collections of me I consider most important . . . You could keep for your heirs the right to publish them in a book whenever they should get my heirs' permission. Your heirs would probably be your daughter Margaret; mine would be Kathleen Morrison and my daughter Lesley.

Your fortitude in the face of approaching death makes it hard not to grant you the permission you ask as a last favor. I am in deep mourning for you. But even so I remain enough myself to shrink from wearing my heart on my sleeve. I say to myself if you can be so sensible about leaving this world it can't be too cruelly much for me to ask you to be sensible about a small matter like these letters. They are even trivial at a time like this. I wonder at your coolness—like Bennen's on the avalanche in Sills' fine poem. If I seem to speak with the least coolness, I have caught the tone from your courage.

Affectionately

Rob"

Margaret died on the 27th of November, 1949, leaving her poems, *Afterglow*, a gay, colorful shawl of thoughts and feelings written throughout the years.

The letters were left to me, true to the sounds of life, true to the people who lived those lives. Spending the afternoon with Frost in Berkeley, California, the day before John F. Kennedy was elected president, we talked of past and present things, of finding one's way and the anxiety in approaching a decision, the overwhelming feelings of not being able to carry through. "Yes," he said. "For fifty years I've given lectures, and every summer I go away from people, hide out in Vermont.

Then in the fall I start the lectures, the talks, and it all comes over me again, the old fears, the anxieties. Why do I do it? I don't have to anymore. I want out, you see, I want out! But then I go on . . . and it's all right." As he walked me to the door, no older than I remembered him as a child, but no longer a big man, for I had grown up tall, he gave me, as he had given my father, a bit of wisdom for a send-off. "And remember," he said, "nothing is momentous. We always think it is, but—nothing is momentous."

Things of the heart live on.

ACKNOWLEDGMENTS   The Bartlett Collection of Frost letters, inscribed first editions, and "Notes on Conversations" have been placed in the C. Waller Barrett Room of the Alderman Library at the University of Virginia. Some of the stories which are quoted appeared in the "Mostly Personal" columns of *The Author and Journalist* magazine, 1943–1948, and are used through the courtesy of Harold Ellithorpe, editor and publisher of the *A&J*. The poems of Margaret A. Bartlett are reproduced by permission of Alan Swallow for Sage Books, Denver, Colorado.

For information which gave substance and depth to my father and mother's New England years, I am indebted to Robert L. Bartlett of Chicago; Ralph Sanborn and Priscilla Roberts of Raymond, New Hampshire; to Charlotte Christian of Derry, who helped with my research; the recollections of members of the Pinkerton Class of 1910, who gave me time when I visited and wrote many helpful letters: Emily Healey Clark, Harriett Healey, the Reverend George Seavey, Clarissa Hall, Myrtle Kelly Taylor, Lillian Sawyer, George B. O'Connor, and Carl and Marion Ladd; the ever-youthful Miss Sylvia Clark, who represented the Pinkerton faculty in the days when Frost was there, and Ivah Hackler, present principal of Pinkerton Academy; Madeline Holland of Groveland, Massauchusetts, who gave me information on the Abbotts.

In Vancouver, British Columbia, I wish to thank those who were helpful in giving me the flavor of the booming, youthful city of fifty years ago: Major J.S. Matthews of the Vancouver City Archives; Beth Edwards and Charles Bayley of the Kerrisdale *Courier;* Alan Morley of the Vancouver *Sun;* Bruce Ramsey, librarian for *The Province;* A.S. Murie, Chief Clerk, Transportation, of the British Columbia Power and Hydro Authority; and Noel Robinson, retired newspaperman.

My brothers, Forrest, John, and Richard, added to my own remembrances of the Colorado years. Research librarians in Colorado and Vancouver were prompt and efficient in searching files in answer to my requests. Earl O. Anderson of Laconia, New Hampshire, furnished me with clippings and letters from his files.

Most of all, I am grateful to Lawrance Thompson of Princeton, who first urged me to "get to work" on the story while I was still snowed under with my own young family. His encouragement and thoughtful criticism have kept me working on the manuscript, sometimes in spite of myself. The good talks with Dr. Richard Greenberg helped me in formulating my ideas of how to handle the material. I couldn't have managed without Fanny Gibbs, who kept the house (and children) under control; the emergency service rendered by my mother-in-law, Rebecca M. Anderson; and through it all, the forbearance of my husband, Samuel T.D. Anderson.

Index